Rambles Through an Alaskan Wild

To those
who can cherish
knowledge of the existence
of Katmai National Monument
without having to go
walk on it . . .

and to the children
everywhere, orphans for whom
the adults of each generation
leave less . . . and less . . .
and less . . .

Rambles Through

an Alaskan Wild:

Katmai and the Valley of the Smokes

Dave Bohn

A Noel Young Book
CAPRA PRESS
Santa Barbara : 1979

Copyright © 1979 by Dave Bohn
All rights reserved.
Printed in the United States of America

The endsheets are reduced from the originals, as painted by JoAnne Clark Popham in the Valley of Ten Thousand Smokes, 1971, primarily from materials found and mixed on site.

The frontispiece is from one of eight watercolors painted during the Alaskan expedition for the Tenth Census (1880), by "WJH." Chromolithographs representing the eight scenes may be found in *Report on the Population, Industries, and Resources of Alaska,* Ivan Petroff, Department of the Interior, Census Office, Wash., D.C. 1884 (Plate II is "Lake Walker, Alaska Peninsula—Mt. Kakhtolinat"). The watercolor artist is not mentioned in the above report, but "WJH" may have been Petroff himself.

The photograph on pp. 82–83 was taken by Michael J. Tollefson, and has been converted from the color slide.

Production acknowledgments: Production assistance by Elizabeth Richman. Imposition and camera work by Larry Bevan, Bruce Shipley and Steve Burns, color separations by Bob Axelsen, presswork by Tony Paszek and Mike Flory—of Haagen Printing. The outstanding darkroom made available by Hilary and Daniel Goldstine.

Library of Congress Cataloging in Publication Data

Bohn, Dave.
   Rambles through an Alaskan wild.

   Bibliography: p.
"A Noel Young book."
1. Katmai National Monument—Description and travel.
2. Bohn, Dave. I. Title.
F912.K3B64   917.98′4   79-14527
ISBN 0-88496-126-5 (lim. ed.)
ISBN 0-88496-125-7

CAPRA PRESS
P.O. Box 2068
Santa Barbara, California 93120

I want Katmai National Monument
to be a place where
the advancement of wisdom
is practiced.

Contents

This is a sketchbook; there is really no beginning to it, and it does not end on any particular page. There are no maps, so don't look for any. For the most part there are no captions, either, though all the photographs were taken within Katmai National Monument and proposed additions. Some of the pieces were written in the field, but most were constructed during the winter of 1977 from extensive field journal notes. Those notes were written all over the Katmai: in tent, cabin, canoe, in front of a fire; in wind, rain and sun—though not too frequently the latter. Rather more often as I cursed the weather.
   As to what this book is about, regardless of what the title may say, I think back several months to a conversation with a good friend who had read the manuscript. He said, "I thought you had in mind a book on Katmai, rather than a book of personal philosophy." I answered by asking—if Katmai National Monument is not philosophy, then what is it? But his query has stayed with me ever since, and I brood over it. Indeed, I hope no reader sees this as a book "on" Katmai.

Foreword

Katmai National Monument is first of all a wilderness landscape, a place where the imprint of wildlife is greater than that of people, where clear lakes and rivers abound, where nearly two hundred miles of coastline bear little sign of man, and where steaming volcanoes rise above the entire scene. It is a land of uncrowded spaciousness, a place where people can experience wilderness on its own terms without the distraction of hordes of other visitors. It is a place where time and change are measured by the sun, the tides, and the seasons rather than clocks and calendars. Katmai, in short, is an experience set in the wild, and perhaps it is even a frame of mind.

Dave Bohn's first visit to Katmai was preliminary and very brief. We met on the beach at Brooks Camp, as he came off the plane, and immediately set out in a kayak to drift the lakeshore together—to get acquainted. The next day we hiked into the Valley of Ten Thousand Smokes, and sat beside Knife Creek to eat lunch. Evenings were spent in my cabin, talking and looking across Naknek Lake to distant mountains. Apparently, the chemistry between Dave and Katmai was already developing, for when he left three days later he said he would almost certainly be back. The Monument had left its impression on him. It will on you, too.

Subsequently, Dave and I shared varied experiences exploring in the Monument. We sat out a windstorm for several days on Grosvenor Lake, watching giant swells roll past our sheltered cove. We camped on the Shelikof Strait in a heavy, unending rainstorm as food ran low and bears strolled past the tent, while waiting for clearing weather and the arrival of our bush pilot. We labored under full packs up a long, hot, shadeless hillside, finally attaining the rim of Kaguyak Crater with its beautiful lake, then camped nearby amidst the ripe blueberries. And we floated rivers together in rafts and kayaks, listening to the sounds of water, wind, and wildlife.

The other side of this book is the author himself, an artist who records not just what he sees, but what he *feels.* The reader may or may not agree with all that Dave says, but will sense that Dave's views are deeply felt and find them thought-provoking. His insights on Katmai reflect the concentration he puts into his work. Once, while Dave and I were kayaking along a shoreline, we stopped so he could photograph ripples and shadows on the sandy lake bottom. As Dave adjusted his camera, a moose stepped from the woods to drink, no more than one hundred feet away. So intense was Dave on his subject matter that he failed to respond to my increasingly insistent nudgings. I very nearly had to hit him with the paddle before he at last became aware of that moose.

Most Americans will never visit Katmai, though they may know that such a place exists. But through the perception and feeling for the Monument presented in this book, they can nevertheless experience the wonders of this national treasure. It is my hope that the reader's inspiration will in some way measure up to what Dave felt as he worked with this land firsthand—a land where man does not dominate, where time and change are measured only by the sun, the tides, and the seasons.

Gilbert E. Blinn, superintendent
Katmai National Monument

Prologue

Allowing for some exceptions, as a species we have not yet done very well with the concept of restraint, either in our relationships with each other or with the rest of the planet, animate and inanimate. We are pillars of stupidity and arrogance in these areas. I don't think there is very much time left for us to learn something about restraint, and I am hardly the first to say that. In the pages that follow, I am primarily concerned with talking about our relationships with land and the other critters on it, although since I am the land and the land is me, I am also talking about relationships with each other and *with ourselves.* (Those who do not respect land have an insidious disease; neither can they respect themselves.)

Thus, I have been doing some wandering out there in the wild, trying to understand more about the aforementioned arrogance, knowing that when we do manage to get beyond it, and when basic needs are not holding us down—it is extremely difficult to be philosophical on an empty stomach—we are capable of magnificent physical and philosophical rapport with land and those other critters. For the most part, however, our rationalized "needs" seem to have seriously obscured this talent; but here and there are signs that we are beginning to see through the mist.

And so, the Katmai. We must learn something about restraint in our approach to this remarkable piece of land, and during my rambles out there I have sifted the concept through many strainers, attended occasionally by clear skies and warm sun, but more often under dark, rumbly skies and cold wind. I continue to sift throughout what follows. Now and then I get a little snarky, and as a result I know I'll lose a few friends and alienate some people I have never met. But I can't help that. It is of supreme importance for Katmai National Monument to exist as it is now, and I must call the shots as I see them.

Not infrequently we hear that old and mindless argument; to set aside public lands as protected (non-commercial) areas constitutes "locking up the land" for the privileged few. Although only military reservations and private lands are truly locked up, those who argue as above are primarily concerned with numbers. It apparently accomplishes nothing to point out to them that the mass recreationist may have $15—25,000 invested in equipment, whereas the backpacker will have $500 invested, so who is privileged? The primary counter-argument will be that when a given area—such as the Katmai—is not made available to "everyone" (through myriad facilities including roads) the process is undemocratic because everyone pays taxes and should therefore be able to *use* the land by walking on it or riding or flying over it. The argument fails badly on at least four counts: only one type of "use" is considered; it is impossible to make all protected areas available to all potential users—that is, there have to be some areas available to the motorcycle or the wheelchair, but there also have to be areas where machines are minimally allowed and, in some cases, barred entirely; we all pay taxes for things we never use directly, but the philosophy is that we gain as individuals because the entire society gains; and finally, all of the preceding arguments are based on arrogance. None of them take into consideration what actions may or may not destroy the land.

We are a mightily inquisitive species, but I think there ought to be some places on earth where every rock does not have to be turned over to see what is underneath. In other words, *leave it alone.* Katmai National Monument should be left alone, but I must explain what I do not mean. I do not mean I see the Katmai as a museum, as a static enclave covering so many square miles. This land and those who live on it are in constant flux. Nor do I believe that human beings necessarily intrude when they enter the Katmai. If alone or with one or two others, you will not intrude, providing you treat the land and the critters with respect—providing you *participate* with the land rather than "use" it as a consumer. The traditional "tourist" can also truly participate with this magnificent land, but only if the numbers are held down. Blatant tourism in the natural areas is violently consumptive and destroys what was there in the first place.

Even though you cannot pick up your telephone and ask a travel agent to arrange a visit to the planet Jupiter, knowledge of the existence of that planet is a gigantic philosophical resource. And, of course, you *can* visit Jupiter once you know it is there . . . with your mind. Thus, I am suggesting that, for the Katmai, the most valuable use by "visitors" will be the knowledge that it is there—that the area remains wild and on its own because only a few go in and those few never intrude.

About fifteen years ago I began to consciously work at sensing a personal philosophy of wilderness ethics. Perhaps ten years ago I was able to start putting some of it into words. And not more than two years ago did I finally understand what I was trying to do with my rambles through the great lands of the Katmai. I was out there somewhere in the wind and space when the old preconscious delivered up the answer; I was trying to find out if there was a way for me to give back to the Katmai more than I was taking away. Given awareness of all the potentially irreconcilable contradictions residing in that desire—such as publishing anything *at all* in reference to Katmai National Monument, I was not sure the premise made any sense. I am still not sure. It remains to be seen.

Unnamed Valley

So far as we know, it was an unnamed Alaskan valley, fifteen miles long and three miles wide, small lakes and ponds, three major stream courses cut deep. Birds, moose, beaver, the small ground animals, brown bear. At the southern terminus of this valley, a twenty-five hundred foot pass through the heart of the Aleutian Range. Across this pass the wind virtually never stops blowing, more often than not a south wind—from the Shelikof Strait. At the northwest end of the valley, drainage turns north and ten miles later reaches a great Alaskan river, the Savonoski.

This valley we are talking about was part of a centuries-old trade route connecting Bristol Bay with Shelikof Strait, an overland distance of about one hundred twenty-five miles, including Naknek Lake. But, in June of 1912, a series of cataclysmic eruptions occurred in the immediate vicinity of the pass, and at some point during these eruptions the valley was inundated by a flow of incandescent ash, probably traveling at least sixty miles an hour, to a varying depth of three to seven hundred feet. The forty square miles covered by the ash flow shortly became a cauldron of vents—hundreds and hundreds of them—as the buried water became steam and combined with gases originating in the flow.

Four years later this valley would receive a name and come to the attention of the world. The name was supplied by Robert Fiske Griggs of the National Geographic Society, who stood awestruck at Katmai Pass on July 31, 1916, looking north across the roaring landscape. And so it became the "Valley of Ten Thousand Smokes."

During the last thirty years of the ancient trade route—Bristol Bay to Katmai village on the Shelikof Strait—a number of travelers went through the unnamed valley and crossed the infamous pass, leaving for us extraordinary though brief accounts. Most of these men, by the time they had reached Pawik (Naknek) on Bristol Bay, were about to cover the final miles of epic sled, foot, and bidarka journeys . . .

Ivan Petrov, special agent for the Tenth Census, under the employ of General Francis A. Walker, left Pawik in late September of 1880, reaching Savonoski village (at head of Iliuk Arm of Naknek Lake, near confluence of the Ukak and Savonoski rivers) on October 3 after a "tempestuous passage" across the inland sea he named "Lake Walker," even though it already had a name—Naknek Lake. From Savonoski, during four days of superb weather, the party pushed through the valley and over Katmai pass to Katmai Bay. A few days later, Petrov crossed Shelikof Strait to Kodiak Island, thus completing his effort on the Census after a journey of twenty-five hundred miles.

In the winter of 1891, an expedition sponsored by *Frank Leslie's Illustrated Newspaper* split in two and the parties traversed about one month apart. The second of these groups was led by Alfred B. Shanz, who left Pawik on February 28 with two sleds, twenty-two dogs, and three native guides. At Savonoski two more guides were hired, and on March 4 the six men and (now) twenty-three animals headed up-valley for the legendary pass. "There, within sight of the notorious pass, through which even now a death-dealing black 'purga' was whirling, we camped, three thousand feet high [more like twenty-two hundred], in the last thin little group of trees."[1] They tried to outwait a blizzard for a day and a half, but Shanz got impatient and wanted to move out on foot without dogs and sleds. The natives thought it would be more prudent to leave one sled behind but take all the dogs. So they did.

> It was a splendid idea. We left everything not absolutely indispensable in the abandoned Esquimau sled on the mountain, hitched the twenty-three dogs to the dainty sled "Cyclone," donned our snow-shoes, and started, at eleven o'clock on the morning of March 7th, on a veritable stampede over the dangerous Katmai pass.[2]

They forced the pass in a violent snowstorm with visibility down to a few yards, but five and a half hours later were at sea level, camped just eight miles from Katmai village.

First to publish the phrase "Katmai pass," historian and astronomer Shanz surely knew how to set it on paper, for throughout the article written for the *Illustrated* his lines fairly crackle with the rigor and excitement of the trail. And in his final paragraphs, one senses what the long journey must have meant to him personally:

> The last day of my sled-travel, March 8th, was begun at an early hour. Spring had so far advanced on this side of the mountains that all the

creeks were open, and we had to make fifteen fords, but eventually we struck a smooth ice-field reaching to the Katmai post, and all six of us sat on the sled and sang an Esquimau chanty, while the twenty-three dogs galloped for the fish-caches. We had been just thirty-nine days on the road, and had traveled eight hundred miles.

My boys took a few days' rest, and afterward left for the north with my beloved dogs, whom I disliked to lose, and who energetically reciprocated my aversion to a separation. But the whips cracked, and the team felt the call of duty, and disappeared in the morning mist which floats grayly over the ice at Katmai.[3]

In the spring of 1898, one of the greatest foot and sled journeys of all time terminated at Katmai Bay. In an attempt to obtain a relief ship for whalers trapped in the ice near Point Barrow, George Fred Tilton undertook fifteen hundred miles overland—Point Barrow to Shelikof Strait, from October 1897 to March of the following year. Tilton made it in fine style, but was rather terse about those last miles on the ground:

From Nushagak [in Bristol Bay] to Katmai we were twenty-one days, striking as hard travelling as we had found anywhere—being in the mountains—and the worst weather. We camped in a blizzard every other day, but we broke camp and got under way every day, even if we only made an hour's run. It was the wind that held us back more than anything. The dogs couldn't stand it at all. When we reached the down slope [the descent from Katmai Pass] it took us three days to lower the dogs and sleds down. Then we started for the beach . . . and in accordance with fate's usual plan we were on the opposite side from the village of Katmai. When we got within sight of the place we hunted up the shoalest spot we could find, hove the dogs in and made 'em haul the sleds across, hanging on ourselves and helping what we could. We made it, but we lost half the camping gear off one sled.[4]

Much to Tilton's dismay, the Alaska Commercial Company's station had been moved out of Katmai months earlier, " . . . there was no grub except game, and not a boat except one old discarded dory that wouldn't hold pumpkins."[5] Pumpkins or

29

no, Tilton had a mission and was not about to quit. He tore the sled apart, saving the sinew lashings. He bored holes in the dory's planking and lashed and sewed the boat together with the sinew. He ripped up " . . . the only suit of underwear that I had on earth and one of my deerskin suits, and caulked her with the rags."[6] At daybreak on March 17, Tilton and his two guides shoved off for the crossing of Shelikof Strait. Tilton rowed the thirty-seven miles to Kodiak Island, never leaving the oars, while his companions never stopped bailing. They made it, and Tilton went on to San Francisco via Portland. Supplies were immediately dispatched for Point Barrow, although by then the stranded whalers had already received partial relief.

In the fall of 1898, Josiah Edward Spurr, a geologist with the U.S. Geological Survey, led a reconnaissance in southwestern Alaska that covered some fifteen hundred miles—by cedar canoe, three-hole bidarka, and finally the Katmai trail on foot. Spurr's group of four (originally seven), plus eight Nushagak natives and one white cannery employee—plus a prospector with his own "bidarky"—entered the Naknek River on October 11, in six bidarkas, escorted in style as far as the lake by an additional six bidarkas from Naknek. At Savonoski, the Nushagak boat crews turned back and paddled for home against lowering temperatures, and ten locals were hired for the trek to the coast. The party reached Katmai village on October 17 without incident, Spurr keeping a geologist's eye on the terrain. As a result, we have the only "detailed" description of the trail, albeit mostly eight pages of geology, but tucked away in Spurr's account is mention of several small events that foreshadowed destiny for an unnamed valley:

> The first 15 miles of the trail from Savonoski to Katmai lies through swampy flats in the broad valley which forms a continuation of the lake. Afterwards a series of rises over slight benches brings one to a larger plateau valley, which, however, is level and generally swampy. The trail lies along this until near the pass, where the plateau valley and the deeper valley of the stream come together. . . .
>   The Katmai pass . . . lies between two volcanoes and is extremely wild and rugged, being the most difficult mountain pass we crossed during the journey. For several miles on both sides of the summit there is no trace of vegetation, the surface being composed of huge angular fragments of rock, piled together without even a covering of moss. Through this debris and

> the underlying lava the mountain streams have cut deep gorges. . . . Extensive hot springs emerge from the Katmai side of the mountains below the pass, and there are very frequent earthquakes and other evidences of volcanic activity. Our party itself experienced a slight earthquake just after crossing.[7]

Petrov, Shanz, Tilton, Spurr . . . these inestimable travelers were by no means the only ones. There are additional accounts, and others traversed but left no written record. And, of course, the natives were using the Katmai trail frequently. If only we had some of *those* stories!

Meanwhile, the Nome gold rush, and by spring of 1899 the trail was being used in reverse direction—that is, Katmai village to Bristol Bay—as some of the prospectors struck for the interior via this route. As to how many stampeders went over Katmai Pass, no reliable estimate seems to exist; and apparently the only published account of any consequence was left by a man who would learn to write, though he would never be given to understatement in his stories. The writer-to-be was none other than Rex Beach who, with a companion, waded ashore at Katmai village in February of 1901, headed for a purported strike (a *big* one) on the upper Kuskokwim River. Forty years after the event, in *Personal Exposures*, Beach devoted seven pages to the trip from Katmai to Savonoski, and they make for wonderful reading. Among other things, Beach started to give out before they reached the crest of the range, so companion Roy Norton prescribed a snort. Two swallows of brandy and Beach was drunk. He clung to the sled as Norton and the guide urged the dogs over the pass in a blizzard, but on the downgrade into the valley Beach stumbled and fell constantly. With darkness coming on, he insisted the others go ahead to the first trees while he would follow the tracks. Scenario for disaster, although Beach made it to camp, if not by much:

> Out of the darkness stunted spruce trees finally loomed, ahead I saw the glow of lantern light shining through a tent wall and heard the sound of an ax. I sprawled through the tent opening, Roy rolled me over and poured hot tea into me.[8]

The next day they went on to Savonoski, picked up some additional dogs, and mushed down Naknek Lake to Bristol Bay, where they learned the Kuskokwim "strike" was bogus:

> Under the circumstances there was nothing for Roy and me to do except continue on to Nome, which we did, acquiring considerable experience on the way. That trip paid me no dividends until years later when I wrote my third novel, *The Silver Horde*. Inasmuch as most of its action occurred in and around the salmon fisheries of Bristol Bay, I was glad indeed that my knowledge of the country had been gained at first hand. . . . On the whole, I profited more from that fake stampede than from any I ever engaged in.[9]

Not long after Beach went through, gold fever subsided and stampeder traffic on the Katmai trail dropped off. The winds continued to pour across the range as usual, but otherwise things were pretty quiet along the traverse. Except beneath the ground in the immediate vicinity of Katmai Pass, and it is unfortunate we have no accounts from, say, the years 1908—1912. The volcanoes must have steamed increasingly, there must have been a rising frequency of minor quakes as pressures rose below and within magma chambers, the hot springs on the south side of the pass must have become hotter . . . and all of these manifestations would have increased sharply as summer of 1912 approached.

Starting about June 1 of that year, earthquakes were consistently noted at Katmai village; and on June 4 and 5, rather severe shocks were felt at distances up to one hundred thirty airline miles from Mt. Katmai, the three-peaked mountain just east of Katmai Pass. On the night of June 5, although the weather was generally fair, observers at Cold Bay (now Puale Bay)—some fifty miles southwest of Katmai village—witnessed a black, stormy northern sky in the direction of Mt. Katmai. And then, according to these same observers at Cold Bay, at 1:00 p.m. on June 6 there was a severe earthquake and a gigantic explosion. At 3:00 p.m. there was another gigantic explosion, this probably the one heard at Juneau, seven hundred fifty miles away.

Explosions combined with rising quake intensity continued throughout the next day, culminating about 10:40 on the night of the 7th with a violent earthquake and, as observed from Kanatak (a few miles below Cold Bay), a tremendous flare of light from the direction of Mt. Katmai, such that "the mountains were like sunshine."[10] Severe explosions, rumbles, and quakes continued through the 8th, and eruptive activity and quakes of generally lessening severity went on through the end of August. But the forty-eight hours commencing at 1:00 p.m. on June 6 were the big ones. During those hours the upper two thousand feet of Mt. Katmai, with its three-peaked summit, disappeared, and the unnamed valley was buried underneath an incandescent ash flow, perhaps on the evening of June 7, starting at 10:40 p.m. as the great flare of light illuminated the mountains "like sunshine." If so, then by 11:00 that evening the forty square miles of the valley actually buried were fiery hell beyond imagining, and the superheated blast of air that must have preceded the leading edge of the ash flow obliterated anything living, well beyond the confines of the final dimensions of the flow.

Within a few days of the eruption, the Research Committee of the National Geographic Society dispatched geologist George Curtis Martin to the area. Martin arrived in Kodiak about July 6 to begin his observations and start collecting eyewitness accounts if possible. All told, Martin spent six weeks in the vicinity, most of it along the Katmai coast. The party returned with extraordinary interviews (and photographs), especially from some of the people at Cold Bay. Before reaching Cold Bay, however, Martin went ashore at Katmai Bay on August 13 and left us this account of the historical village:

> Katmai lies desolate on the edge of the great gray waste. It was fortunate that the people went away before the eruption, for a breath of hell swept down the valley, bringing death even to the trees. The only living things we saw were a few spears of grass, which had pushed up through the places where the wind had swept part of the ash away, and three dogs, who had escaped either by seeking refuge in the inner and deeper recesses of the barabaras or who possibly had been away on a hunt. The scene was the more deathly because it lay on the edge and in full view of the brilliantly green and undevastated country to the west.[11]

Proceeding to Cold Bay, Martin talked with C.L. Boudry, who was in the habit of keeping a diary and had interviewed the last two native families to leave Katmai village. These people evacuated on June 4, only forty-eight hours before the end, and headed southwest in their boat. They were camped about halfway between Katmai and Cold Bay when the great eruptions started. Boudry's subsequent entry, commenting on the stragglers who had just reached the relative safety of Cold Bay, has the eloquence that unpolished accounts so often have:

> They report the Katmy hill blew up and threw rock out to sea, but could

not tel mor as they whare on the road to Cold Bay—an that pommey stone in fire whas falling 20 miles an that the watter was hot in the Katmy bay . . .[12]

As indicated in Martin's account, Katmai village was on the edge of the westernmost heavy fall of ash because of the prevailing winds, which is why the Cold Bay observers saw as much as they did; in other words, the sky above them remained relatively clear. But to the east and northeast of Katmai Bay in areas Martin called the "zone of darkness," the ashfall was tremendous. And out of this zone of darkness came a remarkable letter, addressed to the place Afognak Island, from a Russian native who spent the critical days in a fishing camp at Kaflia Bay, some seventy-five miles up the coast from Katmai village:

Kaflia Bay, June 9, 1912. My Dear Wife Tania: First of all I will let you know of our unlucky voyage. I do not know whether we shall be either alive or well. We are awaiting death at any moment. A mountain has burst near here, so that we are covered with ashes, in some places 10 feet and 6 feet deep. All this began on the 6th of June. Night and day we light lamps. We cannot see the daylight. In a word, it is terrible, and we are expecting death at any moment, and we have no water. All the rivers are covered with ashes. Just ashes mixed with water. Here are darkness and hell, thunder and noise. I do not know whether it is day or night. Vanka will tell you all about it. So kissing and blessing you both, good-bye. Forgive me. Perhaps we shall see each other again. God is merciful. Pray for us.
Your husband, *Ivan Orloff.*
The earth is trembling; it lightens every minute. It is terrible. We are praying.[13]

It is minor historical tragedy that no one managed to collect eyewitness accounts from the other side of the range, from those who had evacuated Savonoski before it was too late. One such interview *was* obtained, in 1918, when Paul Hagelbarger and Jasper Sayre (both with the National Geographic Society expedition of 1917) returned to the valley alone. They went in from Naknek, and while there Hagelbarger interviewed "American Pete," chief of Savonoski village at the time of the eruption. In addition to his barabara at Savonoski, Pete also had one up the Ukak valley about eight miles, or just about at the terminus of the subsequent ash flow. Expecting a disaster because of increasingly severe earthquakes, Pete had been at his up-valley place attempting to remove belongings when hell broke loose. In the last stages of tuberculosis as Hagelbarger spoke with him, Pete was not inclined to say much; nevertheless, his idiomatic English beautifully expressed his impressions—as the only individual known to have directly observed any of the great explosions:

> The Katmai Mountain blow up with lots of fire, and fire come down trail from Katmai with lots of smoke. Me go fast Sabanoski. Everybody get in bidarka. Helluva job! We come Naknek one day; dark; no could see. Hot ash fall. Work like hell. Now I go back every year one month, maybe, after fish all dry, and kill bear. Too bad! Never can go back to Sabanoski to libe again. Everything ash. Good place, too, you bet! Fine trees, lots moose, bear, and deer; lots of fish in front of barabara. No many mosquitoes! Fine church. Fine house. Naknek no good.[14]

It was eventually suggested that what Pete saw was the beginning of the incandescent ash flow, but I think not. If that had been the case, Pete would almost certainly have been caught by the searing wind of death long before reaching Savonoski. As for Pete's lament . . . yes, one can understand that old Savonoski must have been an extraordinary place to live. Trees, moose, fish—and tales immemorial from this superb location on the ancient trade route.

And now July 31, 1916. Robert Griggs, leading the expedition for the National Geographic Society (also the 1915, 1917, and 1919 expeditions), in camp about ten miles above the beach, at the mouth of Mageik Creek in the upper Katmai River valley. A two-day trip across Katmai Pass had been planned, following ascents to the Mt. Katmai caldera on July 19 and 30. But the group was tired from the climb of the previous day and the weather was deteriorating. So they decided on a one-day reconnaissance to the pass—that is, Griggs, Lucius G. Folsom, and Donovan B. Church, the photographer for the 1916 and 1917 expeditions. When near the crest, however, Church apparently decided enough was enough, and was left with the packs while Griggs and Folsom went on. (On the first ascent to the caldera, Church had lugged the big camera, including its twenty-pound tripod. Furthermore, Griggs later claimed that on July 31 Church was "incapacitated by too many flapjacks at breakfast," and thus gave out short of the pass. Flapjacks aside, Griggs highly respected the talented photographer; "He was a youngster whom I had singled out from my classes by reason of his habit of turning up after a field trip with a set of unusual pictures, which he had snapped surreptitiously en route. His genius for seeing pictorial values made him invaluable."[15]

Meanwhile, as Griggs and Folsom approached the pass, they started to encounter ". . . small fissures from which issued half a dozen good-sized jets of steam and perhaps a hundred small ones."[16] Between them and an unobstructed view of the unnamed valley there was one more rise, but it was getting late and Griggs was worried about Church, who had already shivered alone for about four hours. Turning to leave, Griggs caught sight of a distant puff of steam, but the source was obscured by the crest. Fortunately, Griggs yielded to temptation, and he and Folsom walked the final yards to the divide:

> The sight that flashed into view as we surmounted the hillock was one of the most amazing visions ever beheld by mortal eye. The whole valley as far as the eye could reach was full of hundreds, no thousands—literally tens of thousands—of smokes curling up from its fissured floor.
>
> From our position they looked as small as the little fumaroles near by, but realizing something of their distance we knew many of them must be gigantic. Some were sending up columns of steam which rose a thousand feet before dissolving.[17]

Thus, genesis for the idea of a Katmai national reserve occurred about 5:00 p.m. at Katmai Pass, July 31, 1916, and crystallization of the idea came during the long night that followed, as Griggs lay in the tent back at camp, too excited to sleep.

It is very difficult to grasp the depth of emotion Griggs encountered as he briefly explored the steaming valley in 1916, returning in 1917 and 1919 for extensive encampments midst the roaring vents. But if one reads carefully the various articles he wrote for *The National Geographic Magazine* and scrutinizes the truly remarkable photographs, at least some understanding can be gained. As for the written descriptions that attempted an impossible task, I think the photographer D.B. Church nevertheless almost managed the impossible in his impressions of the 1917 effort, written at Griggs's request:

Regardless of our packs, we hurried down the valley, past the few faint, wispy steam jets that mounted from its floor just over the divide, craning to glimpse the first steam cloud to rise from the valley beyond. There floated over the spur of the ridge to the north a billowy cloud that marked the largest steamer.

Reaching the higher ground that had hidden my view, I gazed at the panorama before me. Flanked by Mt. Cerberus and Falling Mountain, spread the valley, a maze of pearly columns that billowed skyward and bent before the strong westerly wind. . . .

The meager pictures of the previous year, and even the graphic descriptions of Griggs and Folsom, had not prepared me to face such a spectacle of awesome magnitude. I had pictured the valley as large; the actual view dwarfed my wildest imagery to insignificance.

I started for the nearest fumarole; it seemed a few hundred yards distant. I found it half a mile away. It was a small fumarole and I crept cautiously up to its edge. From its red-painted throat, which vanished deep in blackness, the sulphur-reeking steam roared forth in a smothering blast.

Passing back, I found a crack in the rock-like crust of the mud-flow, through which sizzled the scorching steam and gas. A few prods with my staff opened a hole into the underground conduit, from which the steam hissed forth. The fragility of the crust and knowledge of the result of a misstep startled me. My fears began to awaken—fears that for several days made me tiptoe over spots where the earth rang hollow beneath my feet. Familiarity gave me greater confidence, but I never ceased to tread carefully the color-daubed regions of subsurface activity.

The next day I began my work in the valley. This day the activity and the interest of work drove fear from me. The one conception that pervaded me was: how like this place to Dante's conception of his "Inferno." It seemed to me, as we stood on the edge of Novarupta, that this was the Devil's own private corner in hell itself. It seemed, as I gazed at the seething steam clouds that rushed from the cooling lava plug, and at the shattered, steam-smothered furnace that filled the rising vale beyond, that there was some vague, fantastic form, a horrid dream, a hideous, potent "thing" which was not for human eyes to see nor human ears to hear.

Then an endless night on the hot, moisture-teeming ground; an endless rolling from side to side to escape the torment of the penetrating heat that seeped up from the hot, sodden ground; and always, as I looked down the valley through the open tent door, shone the marble-like steam columns, which, like tall, writhing specters, swayed in the dim twilight.

There was always a certain awesomeness about the valley which clung to me throughout my stay. I looked forward with relief to the time when I could put from my sight the curling steamy billows that rose from fumaroles and mounted ever skyward.

Pictures cannot bring back the Valley of the Smokes. They have lost the awesomeness that lies in the setting. You may build in memory, but never reproduce, the scenes which lie beyond the Katmai Pass. They seem too big to be a part of the rest of the world. They do not seem to connect up with the little things which are built into our lives.

Outstanding in my memory is the valley as I left it. It was a brilliant day, with puffy silver clouds that floated on a sky of deepest blue and sunlight that glinted on opalescent steam jets and sparkled on peaks fresh-capped with snow.

As, homeward bound, we skirted Cerberus, the steamers turned in the dying sunlight to shimmering gold and the snowy crests of distant mountains glinted yellow. I forgot the heavy pack which bowed my shoulders as I glanced backward at the growing beauty which filled the valley. Through its giant gateway the "Valley of the Ten Thousand Smokes" sank from sight as we dropped over the pass, and the sky above reddened to a crimson halo in the fading rays of the sinking sun.[18]

Well . . . the valley floor is mostly quiet now, but high up on many of the peaks there are active vents, and the craters of Mts. Martin, Mageik, and Trident steam almost constantly, reminding me of another one of the eloquent journal entries from Cold Bay—this one by Jack Lee, dated June 8, 1912, as those last two families from Katmai village arrived:

> They report the top of Katma Mountain blun of. There was a lot of Pummy stone in their dory when they got here and the say Hot Rock was flying all eraund them.

Postscript: It seems that Mt. Katmai collapsed inward rather than blowing its top into the sky; the later-named Novarupta was really the major vent. Regardless, one can hardly improve on "they report the top of Katma Mountain blun of." A beautiful nine-word summary of creation itself.

Notes

1. Alfred B. Shanz, "Our Alaska Expedition...VIII," *Frank Leslie's Illustrated Newspaper,* Nov. 28, 1891, p. 274.
2. Ibid.
3. Ibid.
4. George F. Tilton, *"Cap'n George Fred" Himself* (New York: Doubleday, Doran, 1928), p. 214.
5. Ibid., pp. 214-15.
6. Ibid., p. 215.
7. Josiah E. Spurr, "A Reconnaissance in Southwestern Alaska in 1898," in *USGS Twentieth Annual Report . . . 1898-99,* part VII (Washington, D.C., 1900), pp. 146, 91-2.
8. Rex Beach, *Personal Exposures* (New York: Harper & Brothers, 1940), p. 68.
9. Ibid.
10. George C. Martin, "The Recent Eruption of Katmai Volcano in Alaska," *The National Geographic Magazine,* Feb. 1913, p. 148.
11. Ibid., p. 174.
12. Ibid., p. 147.
13. Ibid., pp. 148, 152.
14. Robert F. Griggs, "Our Greatest National Monument," *The National Geographic Magazine,* Sept. 1921, pp. 225, 227.
15. Robert F. Griggs, *The Valley of Ten Thousand Smokes* (Washington, D.C.: The National Geographic Society, 1922), pp. 189, 72.
16. Ibid., p. 190.
17. Ibid., p. 191.
18. Robert F. Griggs, "The Valley of Ten Thousand Smokes," *The National Geographic Magazine,* Feb. 1918, pp. 153-4.
[19.] The final quotation is from Martin, op. cit., p. 147.

The Valley of Ten Thousand Smokes

The photograph opposite is an aerial of the valley—about fourteen miles from top to bottom—and Katmai Pass is upper right, almost out of the frame.

One can see that there are no "smokes" on the floor of the valley now, but perhaps by a stretch of imagination it is possible to visualize this landscape as a cauldron of steam columns, so exquisitely described by Donovan B. Church from the expeditions of 1916 and 1917. And now by a stretch of the aural imagination add *sound*—the virtually unbelievable roar of hundreds of vents, along with the ever-present smell of sulphur and the constant dampness. Church conjures Dante's inferno, and while this interpretation may seem a bit romantic, I think the comparison is nevertheless justified. Church and Griggs and the others were up against physical, spiritual, and aesthetic experiences such as few human beings are likely to encounter.

If Robert Griggs were alive today and could return to the valley, I am sure that at first he would be saddened. Except for the nearly-incessant wind, he would find silence. The roaring vents are no longer, at least not out on the flats. Memories as intense and magnificent as Griggs carried within can be dangerous baggage, subsequently preventing the acceptance of change. Or even more dangerous because subsequently nothing else can measure up.

Griggs was fated to experience one of the great landscapes in recorded history, yet I have a suspicion that if he returned now, he would in time accept the silence. The valley's days of fiery creation are done, for the geological moment, but the cycle continues as vegetation returns. And since Griggs was a botanist, he would surely appreciate that.

Today, across the landscape of the ash flow, now and then an isolated clump of dwarf fireweed, though very few and far between and only where the "soil" can hold long enough against the wind. And here and there some willow. But I would think that in another hundred years or so the valley floor will be covered with willow and alder—and then the trees will come back. Once we get trees out there, the beaver will return. From the cauldron to beaver, and it really doesn't take very long. Three hundred years, perhaps.

All of the photographs on the next few pages were taken during my first encounter with the Valley of Ten Thousand Smokes—in August of 1973. The weather was magnificent for the first hour, as I entered the valley; and eight days later, during the final two hours of the walk out, I saw the sun again. In between, the valley threw everything at me. It rained and it poured. The dark cloud ceiling fluctuated endlessly between seven hundred and twenty-five hundred feet. There were two duststorms, one of ten hours duration under a forty-knot gale. And there was a night of roaring, violent blackness when the winds were gusting to ninety miles an hour.

During those eight days alone, I nearly went hoarse shouting and cursing at the weather. But that stance was just for show. I knew damn well I would not have had it any other way, and I also knew the photography and I would very probably never be the same again.

In August of 1974 I climbed Mt. Katmai with Susi Tollefson and Helen Miles. But I chose the wrong glacier for a route and, as a result, we hung up among endless ice-cored hummocks of rubble and not a few crevasses. We got through but didn't reach the crater until 5:00 p.m. It seemed best to descend the other glacier, but I knew we were going to run out of light regardless.

Darkness came as we finally got off the ice and entered upon more acres of those ice-cored rubble hills. By the light of the stars we went on and at midnight wound our way out of the last ravine, down into the moat at the snout of the glacier. We were two daylit hours away from the tents but had been moving since seven in the morning and now could not see exactly what was ahead. So we put on every speck of clothing we could muster and lay down on the rubble which was on top of the ice, bivouacked under more stars than I remembered were out there. Fortunately we had no wind, and then the moon came. Although we could just hear the stream at the very base of the glacier, the amount of space we were underneath gave an impression of profound stillness.

At 4:00 a.m. there was a hint in the east. Shortly we were on our way, each with a drink of water and a quarter-section of tropical chocolate bar under our belts. We walked on through the silence of the dawn and as the sun rose above the peaks the tents came in sight. On reaching them we collaborated on a gigantic breakfast. And the profound stillness of our bivouac stayed with us for many days. Indeed, it is with me even as I write.

As evening descended we became increasingly aware of the great snow-covered volcano at the far end of the Valley of Ten Thousand Smokes. Shortly the first star came on and it hovered just above the summit. Since there was no wind we could almost hear the star gain brilliance. But even with no wind it is not as quiet on the top of that peak as you might think. There are roaring fumaroles up there—for Mageik steams constantly, dormant only until the next time.

Walked over the rise and photographed Mageik—hunkered on a sidehill in thirty-knot wind, camera in hand. The summit under fast-moving cloud, Mageik seemed moody. Not so. If anything was moody out there in the space and the wind it was I. No such thing as a mountain with moods.

On a steady bearing toward the steam plumes, now growing larger by the minute, I could see clearly that they were rising from a large rock hummock situated in a saddle between the sheer walls of one of three peaks. At the base of the hummock the sulphurous air was somewhat noxious, but a chill wind from over the summit freshened the stench. Up the brown mud and rock slope I hastened, until within a few yards of the top a roar of ominous nature reached my ears, and I saw that it was actually a *rim* of something I was attaining, not a hummock at all. Peering over the side after a last, cautious step, I beheld a semicircular amphitheater about seventy yards across, whose floor and sides were riddled with more than two dozen steam vents of all sizes, belching in vented discord. The ground all around was discolored by a bilious scale and it was warm and moist beneath my palm. I felt I was touching an open wound in mother earth and that my very presence in such a place of unsettled rawness was a sacrilege.

   Noting that this amphitheater of several dozen fumaroles accounted for only one plume of steam I had seen from a distance, I scurried across to another higher, adjoining ridge, and then once again peered cautiously over a rim. Through swirls of steam and gas my astounded gaze fell on a small lake at the bottom of a precipitous, rock-walled crater. This lake, about forty by fifty yards in area, was an evil, pea-soup green—and boiling. In three different places, huge globular bubbles of the thick green brew were heaving in convulsive bursts. At the far end of the lake, the largest of all the fumaroles I had seen was emitting a solid jet of high pressure steam at least six inches in diameter. From my viewpoint on the rim, the roar from this and additional vents was loud, but down in the crater it must have been deafening.

   With a few more hard looks at the rock crucible, its caustic green contents and swirling steam, I quit this barbarous place and began my long descent toward the little brook far below, with its grass and flowers and gentler life.

Mark Schrader
November 1975

As I rummage through five years of negatives I reminisce about eagles and squirrels, beaver dams and moose, tundra hills and vast lakes, scrub willow, alder, a wild horse, the wind . . . always the wind—and the brown bears. That ancient consideration of a powerful, all-purpose, intelligent, inquisitive, asocial beast. How old that ancient consideration? At least as old as Neanderthal competing for shelter with the cave bears. Which reminds me of 1974, when Ritter and Blinn and I were out on the Katmai coast. We had come down from one of the volcanic craters and were camped on a bench three hundred yards behind the beach. There were trees on three sides of us and across the open section, forty feet in front of the tent, ran a well-defined game trail. Such trails are everywhere in the Katmai except on the snow peaks and on the water. (Actually, big game trails do run through the water but tend not to maintain an outline. That is, a moose can swim long distances though cannot produce much speed. But bears can swim like hell if they really mean business, and only a strong and *fast* human swimmer could possibly pull away, and even then only for a short stretch.)

But that campsite out on the coast. The next morning Ritter wanted to know why I (or Blinn) had been clumping around outside the tent in the middle of the night. Ritter was informed that nobody had gotten up. We all smiled stiffly and went on with breakfast.

In brilliant sunshine I walk down the beach in front of Brooks Camp, for about half a mile, to observe the people-reaction to the tranquilization and relocation operation of mama sow and her three yearlings. This was definitely not something I wanted to see—not any part of it—but was a self-assignment, one that turned out to be the most awful assignment I had ever given myself.

It was not that I had any quarrel with the very difficult decision the National Park Service had made to move these bears to the coast. Mama sow and her yearlings had become increasingly enamored of the campground, and the potential for an incident was growing. The Park Service was on the spot with this one, and had exercised considered judgment. No, I had no quarrel with the decision. In addition to observing the people-reaction to these efforts, however, I wanted to look at the approach to, and the actual routine of, the operation once tranquilization had taken place. So I watched, and as a result was left with an ineffably sour taste, such that on the following day I very nearly folded my tent for a departure from Katmai. Because that Friday afternoon, well down the beach from Brooks Camp, a carnival took place, albeit a small one because there were "only" about twenty-five people there.

In the time-tested tradition of free enterprise (which never knows when to *stop*), some entrepreneur should really have been selling tickets. Damn near everyone there had at least a still camera and, believe it or not, there were two motion picture cameras present. There were some jokes being passed, a rather genial social atmosphere surrounded by a general milling around, a little sunbathing, here and there someone munching on something . . . and back in the trees, just behind the beach, were the four bears flat on the ground, their intelligence and power sedated for now. And then the scientific ritual took place. A tooth was extracted from each bear for age-health determination, the lips were tattooed, and ear fur trimmed and tag attached. (The approach to this ritual was, I thought, very professional and very arrogant. The Park Service was not involved at this point, but I am not trying to be specific here. I am not interested in the one person who performed the ritual. It is the generalization I am after. The ritual-performer symbolized, for me, a mind-set that cannot be laid at the feet of any one individual.)

As I retreated along the beach in brilliant sunshine, the volcanoes shimmering white some forty miles to the south, it occurred to me that the scene I had just witnessed foreshadowed evil winds for the future of both species involved there. As for the bears, they are very shortly (I susupect) not going to have the space they need and will be gone from the planet. They will lose that space because we will see to it, one way or another. But as to *why* we will see to it, part of the answer to that question lies buried within the deceptively simple, carnival-like atmosphere I had observed, as four bears lay paralyzed under the trees just behind the beach, and in the professionally arrogant approach to the ritual mentioned above.

It is extraordinary to watch mama sow rummaging around beneath the falls looking for salmon. Usually, when she first arrives, she wades a short distance, breaks into a run as she nears the deep pool at the base of the falls, then extends her front legs and leaps out of her gait—to come crashing down on the water with a magnificent splash.

At the time some of us were beginning to feel on slightly familiar terms with mama sow, she had three cubs and was the resident bear in the Brooks Camp area. She would bring herself and her children through the surroundings once or twice a day, and one had the notion that she felt at least reasonably comfortable with the indisputable fact that there were human beings scattered around her territory even as she was raising three offspring.

On both sides of this rather amazing proximity, however, things could become nervewracking (I think I can speak for mama here) because the cubs were not overly inclined to keep a strict watch on how close they came to people. And while there are surprisingly many who are ready to think this can be a wonderful experience—to have a cute little brown bear cub waddle up to within five or six feet—nevertheless the honor is not necessarily one that will result in everlasting health for a person. Of course the problem was that mama could have misinterpreted even the most innocent of moves on our part . . . just turning slowly and walking slowly *out of there*, for example, or indeed she could have quite correctly (from her point of view) surmised that you were too damn close to her cub instead of the reverse.

So as I say, it got nervewracking at times, but mama never did get upset at these goings on and stayed in the area. The following year she maintained her residency, and one day I was about two miles out from camp when I saw her with the yearlings. I spoke softly and she sat down. Shortly the yearlings joined her and started nursing. When the session was over she returned to a sitting position, and that is when I made this photograph.

Those of us who remember mama sow from back then are fortunate, I think. If I may be permitted to say so, she was one hell of a bear, keeping her cool as she did.

In rising wind we left the floor of the valley, not far from the headwaters of River Lethe, and climbed straight up the rather steep slope for the crest of the sedimentary Buttress Range. Standing up there in the wind we had Jurassic fossils underfoot and volcanoes across one hundred eighty degrees of vision—some of them steaming—in addition to a parka squirrel objecting (?) strongly at the pass, presumably from near his burrow.

One quarter mile down the other side we saw grass, moss, willow, water . . . so why a parka squirrel living in the barren windswept on top of the Buttress Range, where here and there grows a tiny clump of forget-me-nots and nothing else? Well, I assume there was maximum occupancy lower down and this one was forced to be a pioneer, so to speak. I am inclined to think he won't make it, that near the edge, but he has to try anyway, as long as there is any chance at all, given maximum occupancy lower down. May that unquenchable "trying" never be successfully seen and quantified under the microscope.

We wished him well and descended into the rain.

A cow moose and her rugged-looking calf. They went off through the scrub willow, lifting high their legs. No wonder they can move through that stuff so fast. They don't move through it—they move over it. If I could lift my legs that high, hundreds of acres of scrub willow would not bother me either.

Most of those who come to a wild area such as the Katmai have a tendency to think of the acreage as a giant-scale zoo, and usually there is displeasure in some degree if a bear, a moose, a what-have-you is not seen before the visit is over. The tendency is understandable, but I think we would do well to remember that Katmai is most emphatically *not* a zoo. I don't care what your travel agent or any of the other entrepreneurs told you, those animals are not out there for your pleasure. They are out there making a living and maybe you'll see them and maybe you won't. However, there is no easy answer here. We come out of a culture that has virtually no such thing as a land ethic, and we've been murdering the other creatures for centuries.

So it's no wonder you and I count the snowshoe hares and bears and moose and lynx seen on the way to the Valley of Ten Thousand Smokes. Which is the zoo-approach and how do we get away from it? I confess I don't have many suggestions to make yet, but if you will agree with me that the Katmai is not a zoo and take it from there in your own way, you will have made a start.

The force that drives the salmon to the seemingly fantastic expenditure of energy, as they jump again and again, is manifest in that jump. But I have never seen a photograph of a leaping salmon that expressed anything more than the photographer's awareness that a jump was taking place. What I want to know about is the *salmon's* awareness. So I photographed the falls head on, standing in the middle of the river. But I certainly do not know if I got any closer to what I am after.

I remember two or three discussions at Katmai, initiated by me, on whether or not parka squirrels have a sense of humor. I think this is a weighty question, an affirmative answer to which would be far more important than photography itself, to say the very least. And after looking at the print, I still do think parka squirrels have a sense of humor, and I am about the last person to anthropomorphize.

   The next negative I printed was one of a bald eagle because the train of thought just mentioned led me to remember another wildlife observation I had made, albeit a rather more objective one. I had noticed last year, confirmed this year, that, when sitting on those high branches, bald eagles tend to look at their toes quite often, while emitting squeaky, low-key sounds. To be more precise, I should say they look down in the direction of their toes, and since eagles do not have toes we are talking about claws. I think the low-key squeaky sounds can be reasonably attributed to a feeling of distress at the presence of the human being. But that looking-down business. Why that? On numerous occasions I have observed bald eagles from long distance through binoculars, when the eagle does not know he or she is under scrutiny. Never once, in those cases, were they looking at their toes . . .

Out of the dusk came a wild screeching—a sound out of primeval millenia. What *was* that? A creature meeting death?

One hundred feet away two lynx came up from the creekbed, unaware of the observers. She set herself on the grass and he stood immovable as she screamed at him for at least two minutes.

As dusk became darkness, the two of them wandered off into the trees.

On a wild windswept beach on Shelikof Strait a marsh hawk circled me twenty times at fifteen feet. Inquisitive bird. How do you think, marsh hawk, and what did you think I was?

The arrogance of people-photographers who invade privacy with the camera is, I think, a well-documented phenomenon. Less well considered is the matter of the wildlife photographer, who is just as arrogant as the counterpart, or perhaps more so. More so because, with some exceptions, wildlife cannot strike back, whereas the person whose privacy has been tampered with can attempt to punch the invader in the nose and/or smash the camera. Since I am profoundly concerned with what are the rights of the wild animals, I want to illustrate my point with two stories, both of them actual.

Occasionally, bald eagles will build a nest on the ground on an island. This is a wonderful opportunity for the photographer. Just walk up to the nest and stick the camera right under the beaks of the fledglings. They won't move even if they are capable of getting out. They are under orders not to move. Under such circumstances most adult bald eagles will circle and emit distress cries but they will not actually attack the invader. So the invader, with or without camera, is physically safe and takes advantage accordingly. Thus, a fifty millimeter lens at five feet and the frame jammed with fledglings.

Nevertheless, such arrogance extends well into the situations where physical safety is by no means assured, but this added factor can provide a special dimension for macho, notably with male photographers and when other human beings are watching. Take a cow moose with two calves. On the tundra. In other words, no cover. Three photographers. Two of them definitely content to leave the situation alone, but the third wants to move in. So the third *does* move in. Now mind you . . . this is a cow moose with two children to protect. An adult moose is a very big animal. A healthy adult moose has four extremely functional legs and can move out fast. Very fast. Nor can you bluff your way out of a moose charge by standing your ground, as you can do (statistically) with a bear if there are no alternatives and you have enough guts. The moose will run through you no matter how well you stand your ground.

But to get on with the story, we have the one photographer moving in ever closer, in plain view of mother moose, who becomes increasingly upset at the persistence of arrogance. Suddenly a brown bear heaves into the arena from the opposite direction, having decided to try for one of the calves. No way. The cow runs the bear off, clear out of sight, then returns. However, the photographers shortly perceive that she is not going to stop at the calves but is now charging *all* of them, which unfortunately is exactly what only one of them richly deserves. They scatter in different directions, and the cow rivets her essentially singleminded attention on one of the invaders (the wrong one) and proceeds. From the point of view of the chased, two fortunate elements now come into play. One, he is in good shape and can run for his life for a reasonable distance. And two, the reasonable distance allows him to reach a shallow gully and flatten out. As soon as he is in this position, the cow aborts her justified attempt at murder.

Enough horror stories. The point I wish to make here is that there is no shred of ethical argument which can bestow upon any photographer (or non-photographer) the right to move in as described. Those fledgling bald eagles, on the contrary, have an absolute right not to be hassled. And I do not mean rights grudgingly conferred by *Homo sapiens*. The right is *inherent*, as I have noted elsewhere in these pages. I am not saying no wildlife photographs should ever be taken, but before you go busting out there with your damn camera, consider the following:

1. Excluding the so-called primitive cultures, adult *sapiens* generally exhibit a built-in arrogance toward wild animals. The animals are seen as subjects for observation, elimination, "sport" hunting and fishing, or commercial exploitation. Because of cultural conditioning, there are very few of us who, as adults, can any longer participate with the critters in a landscape. As children most of us were artists on this score, but it is a long, solitary road back to that awareness. Virtually no help is available, although there are signs that changes are coming.
2. When the camera is introduced to the hand, the degree of arrogance increases exponentially as skill with the instrument improves. The same progression can be observed throughout the history of weaponry. Weapons are body extensions which increase power. The camera is a weapon, and photographers have bludgeoned wild animals *because* of this for decades.
3. The critters out there have an inherent right to be left alone—within reason. Enormous restraint is needed. If the only way to get the photograph is by pushing the animal, then the hell with the picture. If that moose is definitely uncomfortable with your proximity, put the

insufferable camera away and increase your distance. She may watch you for half a mile or more, suspicious and immovable, but at least you are delivering your statement of respect by fading into the sunset.

I have come down hard on photographers in the preceding, but have no intention of overlooking the "observational" categories where cameras may not always be part of the arsenal of interference. For example, I include the scientist who seriously annoys wildlife during observation and hangs it all on the peg of advancement-of-knowledge. And finally, to round out my brief sample I mention the organized groups of bird-watchers, who usually roll in from ten to thirty strong—laden with Questars, tape recorders, spotting scopes, cameras, binoculars, field guides, and checklist. They are so incredibly intent on "collecting" birds that they quite literally do not see woods for trees. Elsewhere I have talked about understanding the fact that a wild area such as the Katmai is not a zoo. The bird-watchers haven't figured that out yet, either, but they are not alone in their misunderstanding.

The cigarette manufacturers are now supposed to tell you that cigarettes may kill you. I think the stipulation is reasonable. What about the backpacking and other wilderness equipment manufacturers? There is hardly a one of them that would decline to double or even triple sales overnight, if they could make the stuff fast enough and then market it. But do you realize what all this fancy, piously sold equipment does to wilderness? Pick up one of those euphoric catalogues and you can read plenty about what this or that item is going to do for *you* out there, but I haven't yet seen one of these goddamn wilderness-loving outfits come down squarely on the side of the land—or what is going to be left of it. So I would like very much to see the outdoor equipment manufacturers and retailers take some responsibility, much as scientists do now (sometimes), having learned they cannot put together a hydrogen bomb and hide from the consequences underneath pure research. Just as with the cigarette ads, the backpacking and what-have-you catalogues should carry a warning, perhaps along these lines:

"When large numbers of people enjoy the wilderness using our fine equipment, wilderness is, by definition, destroyed. Therefore, while we are loathe to say it, we must warn you that this catalogue contains a listing of virtually everything you need to rape the wilderness on your own or with a group."

If Katmai is to remain as true wilderness, the large-group zealots have to be kept out. That is, the entrepreneur wilderness lovers—sometimes commercial and sometimes not—who cannot wait to take in eight or twelve or twenty people on the guided canoe trip or the guided hike and you get your meals cooked for you and the whole thing is organized and what better way to see the wild than *organized*, because it is much more efficient to see the wild, guided, than to stumble around in the boonies on your own. As with virtually everything else now, wilderness is packaged, whether or not you have to cook your own meals. But do we need some wild areas where no packages are allowed, where you have to do it on your own, inefficiently? We do. Are there any such areas left? Almost none, but Katmai is one of them. And so it should remain.

I know a fair number of people who are entrepreneur wilderness lovers; some of them are deeply involved in commercial guiding into wild areas, while others operate as volunteers. I have never heard one of them address the question of what happens to the extremely delicate, virtually indefinable philosophical aspect of wilderness when a large group moves through. In other words, it is not possible for the members of such a group to experience what I am talking about but cannot define. It is impossible by definition, once the group size exceeds three or four.

So I say the Katmai should remain as a place where you must do it on your own. No guided trips, no groups larger than six. Preferably only two people and, if you have the experience and skill, go alone. I do not think it too much to ask that there be one great wilderness area in the United States where the indefinable experience can be experienced, where the guidebook mentality will not be able to hand you the shrink-wrapped package to marketed wilderness. The "philosophical" carrying capacity per square mile would be low, of course, and enormous restraint would be required on the part of those who might want to come. But if by not coming, you could be assured that your grandchild would have the opportunity of participating with Katmai in thirty years—Katmai the superb wilderness intact—well, would you buy that?

India has those sacred cows wandering the streets, but of course one can see where the cows are at. Over here we have just as many Sacred Cows, but they are insidious because harder to identify. Take Science. A magnificent occupation; unfortunately, it has become one of the Cows. Certainly there is room for Science in the national parks and monuments, but, depending on the nature of the area, special permits should be viewed with extreme discretion by the National Park Service.

In the wilderness areas such as Katmai, Science should be treated as any other special interest group and *no* such permits should be given. What do I mean by "special permit?" I'll give two examples: Science loves to collect "specimens," but unless unusual circumstances exist, specimen-collecting is the same as *hunting*. Since Katmai is a national monument, it is understood there is to be no hunting, and that should go for Science as well as you and me.

The second example has to do with Science's equipment, and I will build a composite scenario. Let us say you have saved for six years in order to afford your dream safari to the Katmai. You are traveling as a party of one and intend to spend about four days alone in the Valley of Ten Thousand Smokes. At Brooks Camp campground, you eat Velveeta cheese and Wonderbread sandwiches so as to save the backpacking food. Then comes the great day when you leave the overlook at the lower end of the valley—you are now twenty-two miles from Brooks Camp—and head southeast toward the volcanoes, alone in a moonlike landscape of inestimable beauty. Seven hours later you are nearing the upper end of the valley, tired and about ready to camp, though beginning (*just* beginning) to know silences you have never heard of. And at this moment a Cessna 180 arrives—the first of three such flights, perhaps—with geophysicist and seismological equipment aboard, ready to conduct research for one month. The Cessna lands five hundred feet from you and would you care to make a few comments for the record?

The Valley of Ten Thousand Smokes is a fine place for geophysics and I am all for it. But no Sacred Cows. If Science needs equipment in there, let them pack it in or else not go in at all. And do not be fooled by that pious old saw, the "advancement of knowledge," as if knowledge should be equated with the gross national product. Pursuit of the advancement of knowledge certainly keeps scientists off the street but, as with everything else, there is a point at which the game becomes essentially self-serving. We have been self-consciously advancing knowledge for several centuries now, most recently on a logarithmic curve, and still I am waiting for something else to settle out. In other words, Katmai National Monument is a place where we can practice the advancement of wisdom, and I would like to see Science get in the act.

If you are a backpacker with a good pair of legs and can go into Katmai alone or with one or two others, your gain is on behalf of all of us. When you can no longer do it on your own, however, don't ask for a road across the Valley of Ten Thousand Smokes or a chairlift to the top of Mt. Katolinat. Instead, pass on the philosophical space to someone else, and in this way the whole of it is not lost. And don't tell me I want to "lock up" Katmai (as designated Wilderness, that is) for myself because at the moment I have the legs and can get in there alone. Such an argument is petulant and weak-minded. I do not want to see anything "locked up," and furthermore, the label is meaningless when applied to public lands. There are hundreds of places where backpackers can see hundreds of other backpackers, but shortly there will be no place anywhere where a backpacker might not see another one for two weeks.

And you tourists. There are hundreds of places where you can stay in posh surroundings and watch thousands of other tourists. Don't ask for that here. Katmai is wild country, not a spa. You come to Katmai because it is something else. That something else will be destroyed for *everyone* (that especially includes the bears) if too many of you come and if you ask for additional facilities. Additional facilities is self-fulfilling prophecy to assure that too many will come.

If Katmai is to remain wild as it is now, then the philosophical carrying capacity—that is, physical visitation—must remain low. The old, idiotic yardstick of "visitor use" must be discarded for this wilderness area. Otherwise the uniqueness of the Katmai will be destroyed, and the potential of that gigantic philosophical resource—the knowledge that it is there—will also disappear. Restraint. In the Katmai, we need to practice the kind of restraint we have scarcely articulated.

I am not talking here about catching a fish or shooting a moose and eating it. Depending on where these activities may take place and given the necessary limitations, obtaining one's food in this manner is absolutely legitimate.

Many fisherpeople come to Katmai, and if you observe them for very long, you can begin to believe so-called "civilized" human beings exhibit a streak of pure savagery that is unaccountable. I am not talking about those who fish for the pot, although I question whether the Katmai visitor should be allowed to fish and transport the catch elsewhere. However, for the moment I want to look at those who fish for "sport" (whatever that may mean), and I will suggest two categories:

1. Those who think they *must* fish when they get to Brooks Camp, even though they have not the slightest intention of eating anything they might catch. Furthermore, when they get the fish on the beach they don't know what the hell to do with it and they don't want to get their hands dirty so they step on flopping fish with one foot, tear out the hook by pulling on the line or else ask some other fisherperson to get the hook out and then kick the fish back into the water where it will die because it has been on the beach for too many minutes and the injury is too severe. This scenario, incidentally, is not only accurate but is enacted dozens and dozens of times every summer at Brooks Camp.

2. The other group I have in mind includes those who practice the fine art of what is called "catch-and-release." In other words, the enjoyment comes primarily from knowing how and where to throw the hook, and then in expertly playing the fish on a low-test line, while the fish fights for its life. Having expertly played and landed the catch, one then removes

the hook carefully and quickly and returns the injured animal to the water. Unless it is a trophy fish, of course. Since by definition the fish is injured as soon as it takes the hook, what interests me here is the psychology of pleasure ("sport") that attends playing with an injured animal on a string. I have a dark suspicion that this psychology, if written out on paper, would not make for pleasant reading.

Sportfishing in the Katmai, and anywhere else for that matter, is an abomination and should be abolished. It is an insult to the intelligence, to the Katmai itself, and to the memory of those who fished the Brooks River *for food* almost four thousand years ago and until recent times.

The crux of the matter is ethics. Once we became capable of ethics, the land itself and the other critters out there gained rights vis-à-vis human beings. Again, I am not talking about fishing or hunting for the pot. But if you sportfish (or trophy hunt) you are not an ethical animal, period. Also absurd is the practice of tourist or camper freezing a catch for shipment out of Katmai. There is something inherently pitiful about coming from many hundreds of miles away, catching a "legal" limit in one of the most magnificent of the remaining wild areas on the planet, and then taking the fish home on a Boeing 707.

But I wonder about fishing for the pot in Katmai. For a camper to take a fish that is eaten immediately (which is already done), or for the tourist to take a fish that would become part of the family-style evening meal on certain days of the week . . . I think this might work.

In earlier days, not much more than a hundred years ago in America, for example, there were still some blank spots on the maps. Areas lacking detail. Now and then a vague squiggle suggesting a river or a mountain, but mainly guesswork. Rumor. Watercourses not worked out. Unknown peaks. That is, not just unnamed peaks; *unknown* peaks as far as the mapmakers or the Mountain Men were concerned. (Of course, I am speaking of the Invaders who landed at Plymouth Rock and eventually thronged westward and inundated a continent. The original inhabitants had known at least some of the unknown peaks for ten thousand years.)

Those blank spots on the maps—and certainly not only in America—were a magnificent philosophical resource. I do not think any who canoed, walked, or sailed into the unknown came up with such a self-conscious phrase. Yet, they knew. But now, no more blank spots on earth maps. We have them again elsewhere, as the maps of Moon and Mars begin to fill in. And then Mercury and Saturn. And outer space? But on earth maps everything is verified squiggle.

Perhaps on the map of the United States we could re-color some areas. Remove the verified squiggles and substitute a white spot. I know this would horrify mapmakers and guidebookers of today, who are very tidy-minded and get uneasy when any feature is left unnamed, let alone unknown. But mapmakers, guidebookers, and other tidy-minds aside for the moment, imagine deliberately setting out to enter a white spot on the map. No squiggles, no names. You do not know what is in there. By agreement, no one photographs in the area and no one writes about it. I do not mean you are told you cannot take a camera along. What I mean is—you do not *want* to take a camera or notebook because you want to be sure the white spot remains for yourself and especially for others. It would also be agreed that you would be truly on your own if you went in there. Somebody might come look for you if you didn't eventually show, but they might not. And if you set your tent on top of a bear and got mauled, you could not sue the U.S. National Park Service for negligence.

Well I for one do not think we will put any white spots back on the maps. Too many tidy-minds around. Assiduously we pursue the unknown and in our righteousness about our right to know, wonder and respect get trampled. I suspect the tidy-minds have already taken over the planet. But perhaps only for a time. Meanwhile, I will have to buy a white crayon and color my own blank spots on the map of Katmai National Monument.

There are certain parts of the Katmai I shall never see because I do not want to turn over every one of those rocks to find what is underneath. But as I have rambled through some of the other places—on foot, in a canoe, occasionally in the air—I have become increasingly aware of the importance of beaver in the natural cycle. They alter very large tracts of land out there. What an incredible animal.

Later in the day I was thinking about the size of the universe contained in that superb nest, surely the most beautiful robin's nest I had ever seen. (The space-time represented in the architecture of that nest was enormous. So the nest became part of a solar system; at the center, and all else revolving around it.) And then, as I was wrestling the camera into position, a man came down the trail and wanted to know what I had. On being told, he allowed that he and his wife had found a nest with eggs in it, up the trail aways. It would be nicer, he thought, to photograph a nest with eggs than without. But in the solar system I was seeing at that moment, I didn't need any redundant eggs muddying the issue. Nor any robins, either.

   A few days after the robin's nest, an extraordinary day with beaver dams. There must have been eight or ten dams scattered over a dozen acres. Prodigious amount of work involved. The beavers were gone because their food supply had drowned. Eventually the dams will break, the earlier vegetation will come back, and so will the beavers. As I was photographing I realized that, given the choice between making a picture of a beaver or a beaver dam, I would not hesitate. The dam states exquisitely what the beaver *has* to be. I cannot imagine ever again seeing an area that would more eloquently express the beavers' universe.

   Not a beaver to be seen.

Floating the lower Headwaters Creek in muggy heat and ferocious bugs. Ten-foot banks. Could be an African river except for those spruce sweepers on the edges of long meanders. Expect to see water buffalo any moment. But, no water buffalo. Nor any moose, either. Only a geranium or two. I am grumbling about not seeing much to photograph, but why? I certainly don't need to bring back photographs every time. But I'm learning more about this problem. Each succeeding year in the Katmai

I am less aware the cameras are with me. One of these days, I tell myself, I'll head out from Brooks Camp without the cameras—at last. Meanwhile, back here on the river the heat is about the same and the bugs are driving us crazy. Is that a water buffalo over there in the alder?

In 1919, Robert Griggs of the National Geographic Society named the Savonoski River after the abandoned Savonoski village, originally situated at the confluence of the Ukak and Savonoski rivers. Year-round habitation in the immediate area of the confluence probably dated from 1500 A.D., and permanent evacuation of the more recent village sites (there were two settlements) took place not many hours before the final, cataclysmic eruptions of 1912. Origin of the placename "Savonoski" is not known with certainty. During the Russian period, the name "Seviernovsk" (bestowed by the Russian monk Savonof?) was applied to the two settlements, although the natives called the place "Ikkaghmiut."

The Savonoski River. Its headwaters are frozen—frozen rivers coming down from the volcanic summits. The Savonoski flows braided and it is not easy to keep track of the main channel. The valley is miles wide and flat, and the peaks surround. Moose and bear drift across the bars. Bald eagle flying high . . . watches. Lynx. Great grey owls. Cut-banks, sweepers, snags. Great Alaskan glacier-fed river, muddy. Easing across riffles and through eddies . . . a brown bear just stood up to see who but did not like the answer given by the wind. Sun, rain, and always wind on the Seviernovsk, surrounded by immensities of space.

We were on Grosvenor Lake and it was flat calm. But the wind came up fast as it so often does in the Katmai. And a headwind at that. So we kept an eye out for a lee beach and paddled in there to wait. We waited the rest of the afternoon but the winds got bigger. The tents were set in high grass among the birches and as the air roared overhead we sat around our little fire and swapped wilderness lies until midnight. The incredible thing was that even though it was blowing thirty from the east we didn't feel a breath on that tiny beach.

The next day all day it blew forty and occasionally one of us would walk over to windward and watch the waves crashing against the rocks below the cliff. From there you could see the east end of the lake and mostly it looked like more wind coming down from the peaks beyond.

On the third day it was calm at dawn. We loaded the boats and paddled away silently. Not a one of us will ever forget that place and those hours—holed up on a tiny lee beach while it roared forty above the trees and across the water.

It was only 3:30 in the afternoon and I wanted to move for another two hours. But that dark, rumbly looking stuff over the peaks was coming on fast and wind was already high and rising. I was at the last grove of willows. No more trees of any consequence up-valley, mainly bushes. So I decided to dig in. What with all that air blowing around, it took an hour to set the tent—lashed to the trees and two hundred pounds of rocks on the guylines. As I crawled in, the rain hit. Nearly horizontal rain but not quite. By 9:00 the rain started to ease, and I suspected that meant bigger wind. It did. At worst, I think it was gusting fifty-five knots.

Wind country. You set your tent in this country anywhere you can't handle sixty within half an hour . . . Well, we all make mistakes. When I headed out the next morning, I took care to thank my friends.

I want to know if a tree—any tree—really wants to be photographed. I have asked numerous trees this question but am not yet very clear on the answer. I like to think, however, that if the photographing is done with sufficient respect, privacy will not be invaded. In fact, if photographed in a certain way, perhaps the tree can speak through the print, will be glad to have the chance, and will have something important to say. But what is the "certain way" to photograph a tree? I was hoping the question would not be asked because it is so difficult, if not impossible, to answer. In an attempt to speak for the tree, nevertheless, my answer would run about like this:

At first trees are photographed as trees, but since the photographer is self-conscious with the camera equipment and has not bothered to make any attempt to win the trees' confidence, the results are a mess. Next step comes when the photographer has gained considerable skill with the equipment and has started to philosophize. At this stage it is *de rigueur* to photograph trees so that they look like anything but. Thus, nothing at all is said about trees, nor can the tree say anything, either. Third step comes when the photographer has gotten rid of all the heavy stuff, is at ease with the equipment, and has started to make serious attempts to gain trust. *Now* the tree is able to come across in the print and say quite forcefully and proudly, "I am a tree." That is an important statement, to be sure, but if I understand my friends (the trees) correctly, they are wishing to say something more, something of inestimable importance. What they truly wish to say to you and me is, "I AM THE UNIVERSE."

I know I have a long way to go before my friends will be satisfied the message is being communicated adequately, but I have told them in no uncertain terms that I am trying, and *have* been trying for a long time.

Katmai's Wild Horse

Amalik Bay is possibly the most beautiful of all bays on the Katmai coast. Cliffs rise direct from the water in many places, to alder-choked benches and thence to steep slopes and more cliffs, at last to the peaks which often disappear into the clouds. And rock beaches. Exquisite rock beaches on all the smaller islands. Then, not too far back from Takli Island, which lies at the entrance to Amalik . . . a peninsula. This peninsula has a narrow neck but widens out to one half mile and is one mile long, thick with alder and willow and bear trails connecting sporadic sand patches. In fact, there are trails everywhere in Amalik Bay, including the islands. Trails used for centuries by the brown bear, moose, occasionally wolves and, presumably, even more occasionally by the wolverine.

During the season, now and then a fishing boat anchors near the neck of the peninsula, protected from the open waters of Shelikof Strait by the geography of Amalik. But not very often such visitors. During the months of winter snow lies deep and the wind moves with enormous strength, though again, the peninsula is somewhat protected from the worst of it. At that time of year there are no visitors whatsoever, not even to the peninsula. So it can be said that, with the exception of the small ground animals such as squirrels, Amalik had never hosted year-round habitation, for even prehistoric occupancy of Takli Island—reaching back periodically for about six thousand years—had probably been seasonal. Yet, by spring of the year 1957, the people living in places known as Kodiak and King Salmon learned that Amalik Bay had gained its first permanent inhabitant ever: a horse.

Apparently, in summer of 1956, a group of about sixteen horses were leased out for oil exploration work near Becharof Lake. In September, after the seasonal effort was completed, the horses were being hauled to Kodiak on a barge. But the barge had been slightly damaged at the Puale Bay landing site, and began to ship water as the Shelikof Strait weather deteriorated with customary speed. So the skipper put in to Amalik Bay, the horses were chased ashore, and the barge went on to Kodiak. At this point, the story splits into three versions: the owners went back some weeks later and rounded up the horses, but could not find the sixteenth; fearing the horses would starve but unable to return with the barge, they went back and shot them, but could not find the sixteenth; the owners were unable to return that fall and the horses died during the winter—except for a bay gelding.

As chance would have it, the horse's peninsula provided him with what he needed. Ample grass near the beaches, salt, fresh water streamlets in summer, and the sand patches which he frequented. Bears and wolves must have treated him as a moose; that is, they sized him up and knew he was healthy and could kick the hell out of them. So they left him alone, and the years passed. The occasional visiting fishermen often saw him, and one or two of them would periodically leave him carrots or lettuce, but could never persuade him to feed from the hand. As a rule, no one got closer than one hundred and fifty feet. Subsequently, as fascination with the tale grew, low-flying pilots would check the peninsula to see if he was alive and well, and on return to King Salmon or Kodiak the question was inevitable: "Did you see the horse?"

Katmai's wild horse, in other words, had become a living legend.

In August of 1973 I flew to Amalik Bay, a ground party of one searching for a wild horse on a brush-covered peninsula. (At Katmai only four days the previous summer, I heard the story and then worried for months; the famous gelding was in his sixteenth summer out there, and would he get through another winter? I had become obsessed with the desire to meet the living legend on the ground and, with his permission, perhaps to make a photograph of him.) As we came in low over the peninsula, the creature was down there just where he was supposed to be, sunning himself at one of his favorite sand patches.

The rest of that day and all the next, I roamed the horse-bear alder trails, crossed sand patches and stood on knolls with binoculars. In roasting sun I climbed a miserably steep, rocky, dry stream course, with utmost attention to the devil's club, until I was eight hundred feet up and could see clearly all of the near half of the peninsula. Nothing. No bears, no moose, not even a horse. Only sea gulls on the tide flats. Soaked from perspiration and followed incessantly by a cloud of insects, I descended and spent another two hours on the trails. It was becoming obvious I could spend a month and never succeed in meeting the critter on the ground.

I was out early the next morning. The sky was clear and the grass knee-high wet. A very long day was anticipated. But then, as I was about to emerge from the alder onto sand patch number two, I met Katmai's wild horse. He was sixty feet from me, lying faced away. I was partially screened by the brush and he gave no sign he had heard me. However, as I eased the pack off, he got up very slowly and ambled out of sight. It took me two minutes to fit the silly camera with telephoto lens. Then I stepped out from the alder, whistling softly. (It seemed absurd to be whistling Sibelius' "Valse triste" to a horse, but I had decided on music rather than talk; and besides, I doubt if "Valse triste" on a peninsula in Amalik Bay is any more absurd than searching for a wild horse across bear trails on a peninsula in Amalik Bay.) The living legend shortly ambled back into view at the other end of the sand patch, came forward until he was about seventy-five feet from me, and for five minutes we two stood there looking at each other. Then he departed.

I remember waking up this particular morning, aware that I had dreamt of seeing the horse and singing "Home On the Range" to him. He was below me as I stood on a little bluff, and he looked up at me once with great big eyes. In the dream, I never got a picture because it took so long to get the camera ready; I couldn't operate the lens properly because I had never seen it before. But now I sit here in the grass, where I stood a few moments ago with camera. I did not go after him. I am still whistling. I think one does not very often meet a living legend.

The following day about noon, now with Ward Hulbert and Pat and Marilyn Connor, I went across the tide flat at the rear of the peninsula. At one quarter mile we spotted him grazing near the beach. At five hundred feet he quit eating and came out on the flat to look us over. For half an hour, at about two hundred feet, we talked with him. Ward was filming 16mm color, and I managed just one good portrait, I thought, as he stayed in the same spot for fifteen minutes. (Since the wild one had come across the sand to more or less meet us halfway, I had to assume we had permission for the photography.) When he had had enough he walked slowly toward the grass, then galloped off into the alder. I was around for another six days but did not see him again.

Goodbye wild horse. I wanted to fly over as I left, for a last look at you, but in worsening weather minutes counted. Goodbye wild horse and may you continue to prosper the rest of the summer and may you have a calm fall and not a hard winter as you wander slowly and with musical grace across the countless trails you and the bears have worn through the brush of your peninsula. As you enter upon your eighteenth year of residence, when the end comes may it come in some wild, quick way. It was a privilege to be near you. Goodbye wild horse of the Katmai.

During summer 1974, the National Park Service flew its normal aerial patrols along the Katmai coast, but no one aboard any of those flights was catching sight of the gelding. As I left Katmai in mid-September, I telephoned Kodiak and talked to several Fish and Game personnel, at least one of whom had seen the horse in the spring. Additional names were passed to me, and eventually I reached Mrs. Jay Gallagher. She said Jay would be returning with his boat that night. Two days later, he reached me in Anchorage.

When Jay anchored near the peninsula in mid-April, the horse had come down to the beach, apparently in good shape after the winter. Jay left some delicacies. But when Jay visited Amalik Bay again about a month later, he found the horse's bones, surrounded by tracks of about eight wolves. So our telephone conversation lengthened out a bit as Gallagher spoke with obvious affection:

> I knew him since 1962. I'd take cabbage and carrots to him whenever I went over to fish Dungeness. I'd anchor in there every night. He would hear the boat engine and run down to the beach. Until about two years ago I could get real close to him, about four or five feet, but by 1971 or 1972 he would stay off some distance. But he would never let me touch him. Only time I did try to touch him, in 1965, he tried to nip me. When I'd hold out the food, he'd put his head forward and his nostrils would flare, but he wouldn't take from the hand. He'd step back maybe eight or ten feet, and then would eat what I set down, watching all the while to see I didn't try to catch him.
>
> His teeth were good and his hooves must have been trimmed by the

rocks. Probably weighed nine hundred pounds until he started losing weight about 1971, and he never really got "fat" again. The bears didn't bother him and he wasn't scared of them, either.

I found his backbone, ribs, neckbone, one leg with hipbone, but no skull. Wolves. As near as I could tell, there'd been eight wolves around there. Like I say, that's the first time I'd ever seen wolves over there, but I know now that others had seen them elsewhere on that coast. Might have been around April 20th, but could have been as late as early June. So far as I know, he was seven years old when put ashore, so he was in his twenty-fifth year when he died.

Katmai's wild horse — Amalik Bay, August 1973

Thus the story of Katmai's wild horse. Bay gelding with dark mane and tail to match. Slim white streak down the nose. Shiny coat as if brushed every day. Alone of his kind out there. Legendary creature of a peninsula in Amalik Bay.

In the late evening of the first of August, 1976, there was a remarkable gathering in the lodge at Brooks Camp. All those staying at campground attended, as well as all National Park Service staff and some of concessioner staff. Primarily, the subject to be discussed was a very specific one; necessary limitations on the number of sites in the campground. But as the group began to loosen up under Mike Tollefson's (NPS) low-key manner, the discussion edged beyond specifics and many of the campers and concessioner staff began to talk of what Katmai *is*—by sharing their own experiences. Perhaps fifteen or twenty people spoke, and the curve of eloquence ascended steadily as the evening progressed, although the first person Tollefson called on dished out the same manure we have waded in for a century; namely, that the Katmai was in no danger of being overrun with people now or in foreseeable future, so why even discuss such matters? But this "lecture" was not purchased by the other forty people in the room.

As subsequent speakers weighed in, it became apparent that every one of them was walking through a personal door to say the same thing . . . all of them had been profoundly moved by the Katmai, and were saying that they understood how easily this wild could be destroyed if the visitation were to get out of hand. These individuals were transcending the usual verbalization of short-term interest and expressing an almost intuitive understanding of what is at stake in Katmai.

At the center of all this was Tollefson, who sensed when a speaker was about to come out with something important but needed the encouragement of a question. Finally, at a very late hour, a woman who had not previously entered the discussion (sitting on the floor with husband and child) talked about what they had experienced in their three-day visit. She also wanted to express thanks for what had *not* been destroyed, and she wanted some assurance there was a chance for Katmai National Monument to be shielded against the type of visitor use that would kill the intangibles she was trying to articulate. She was somewhat shy and uncertain of her choice of words, but was reaching for something big. Tollefson probed slightly, with a question or two, and in the last exchange of the evening this woman spoke *directly to Katmai,* with extraordinary simplicity:

(Tollefson first) "Are you coming back next year?"

"I would like to."

"Would you agree with the suggested restraints on visitor uses if this would assure Katmai remaining wild?"

"Yes, I would agree."

"Suppose this would mean you should not come back here for ten years?"

"Well . . . well, I had not thought of that. Well . . . I guess I would have to say I would be willing not to come back for ten years if that would allow others to experience this wilderness."

Five hundred yards away, at the back of the cove, was a squiggle in the shoreline that suggested stream entry. Also something very white in there, directly in front of the squiggle, it seemed. Odd? Wasn't sure. But since the plan was to somehow become part of a salmon run for one morning, we paddled silently toward the narrow beach to investigate. Indeed, when still three hundred feet out we saw dozens of fins breaking surface just offshore. Salmon. So it *was* a stream, a tiny stream entering Bay of Islands, and the something white turned out to be a moose rack at the edge of the water. Because we wanted to participate (is it really possible to do so?) and not invade, we landed the canvas boat two hundred feet away and walked slowly and quietly over to what was, at least for two human beings, an incredible scene.

There must have been fifty red salmon inside a minuscule lagoon—most of them bunched closely with snouts above water, the remainder scattered around in varying degrees of weakness, including a pair that had navigated the twenty feet of streambed to the rocks (which was as far as they could go) and were almost imperceptibly moving to stay with the slight current, but so near death they had little movement left in them. Outside the one-foot-deep lagoon, in the lake proper, were another fifty or sixty salmon, milling. Scattered on the sand and across the bottom of the lagoon, some half out of the water, were another forty in varying stages of decay. And the moose rack with skull, at the interface of land, water, sky, living and dead salmon. The scene was so extraordinary we whispered, though hardly even that, for there was nothing that needed saying.

Perhaps it would have been better not to take any photographs. I was equivocal then about doing so, and do not ever expect to fully resolve the issue, given such circumstances. Too often, I fear, the camera is used automatically and compulsively to collect images, and the millions of negatives that result are analogous to those window decals vacationers plaster on their automobiles; twenty-five National Parks visited in fourteen days. In other words, with that goddamned camera stuck in front of an eyeball, how much do we really *see*? Or for most of those photographs are we just looking and collecting? And in any event, would it be possible to put on film even the slightest bit of the intensity of this scene? Doubtful, knowing that no subsequent print could ever reproduce the sound of the very small stream, the slight rustling of the wind in the trees, and the stench.

As we left two hours later, I know I was aware of the eloquence of what we had come upon, but I also remember we subsequently referred to it as the "death scene." Such a label rankled, however. More of that anthropomorphism which is so hard to dump, combined with the shortrange viewpoint. Still, there was a handle missing. I wanted very much to know why we had been so overwhelmed by what we had seen, feeling absolutely sure that some dead and dying fish were merely the tip of the iceberg.

More than two years later the answer finally came. At a distance of a few feet, that morning at the back of the cove, we had witnessed the explosion of a star. Death scene? Hell no. Those salmon had been gone five years but they had returned—to pass it along. We had stumbled onto a small yet infinite stage, explosive with the power of lifeforce, manifested there by salmon holding to a genuinely predestined rendezvous—a rendezvous with *life*; and the energy that had driven them for five years and was being passed on was every bit as powerful as the energy that blows the chemistry of a star across the light years.

I have been convinced for years that visual anthropomorphism is destructive. I have mentioned elsewhere that it took me a long time to understand that a moose is a volcano and vice versa, but I don't think it's the same thing when somebody looks at a cloud or a rock and sees a human face in there. I just can't believe you will ever begin to learn what the hell a rock is if you are busy with that little game. Indeed, rocks and clouds and human beings have much in common, but I know that as soon as you lay a face on a cloud, your chances of being a cloud are gone, because you are so damn busy talking about yourself you won't hear a thing.

With the written word the same problem occurs. I remember reading somewhere that a brown bear had jumped "gleefully" into a stream choked with salmon. Maybe you feel philosophically closer to the bear if you apply such a word, but not so. Such anthropomorphic self-consciousness just traps you on your side of the zoo; as soon as you inform that bear he or she was gleeful, you have erected a large barrier between yourself and the critter, as if the difficulty of understanding a bear is not already great enough. The point is, the barrier gets much higher when you tell a bear stuff like that because what you are really doing is trying to cut the bear down to manageable philosophical size by assigning motivations you can understand. And you end up understanding nothing.

We do the same thing when we lay names on the landscape. Take that steaming peak out there in the Katmai. Unnamed and therefore especially "mysterious." Can't have that, so somebody rushes to the Board on Geographic Names and makes a suggestion. Two things here: one, the somebody gets a boost for the ego by naming the peak; and two, as soon as the peak is named it becomes much less "mysterious," much easier to manage, so to speak. In fact, what a great way to kill wilderness, by naming every feature in sight. I have not a few friends who for years have been traveling in the wild and the list of placenames they have submitted is shameful. Far too many of those names have been accepted. But the outstanding record by far on this sort of thing must surely belong to the USGS. For decades, *that* outfit has murdered wilderness wholesale with all the naming they have done.

    Fortunately, in the Katmai there are still many geographical features unnamed, and they should damn well stay that way. Nevertheless, the Katmai has also been fortunate with the placenames that have stuck. An extremely high percentage are native, though sadly we have translations for only two or three. The natives generally named locales rather than specific features, and one can hear music when translation is available. For example, the white man came on with the names Brooks Lake and Brooks River, both of them submitted in 1919 by Robert F. Griggs, who failed to obtain many of the native placenames during his expeditions into Katmai. But what was the native name for the locale just mentioned? It was—and still is—*Kitivik*, which translated supposedly means

> *Beavers broke their houses*
> *a long time ago.*

A wilderness string quartet in just eight words.

All of us are pack rats and I assume we have been for several million years, or ever since we decided to stand up. So here and there around the study I have an old moose mandible, some rocks, pumice, a snowshoe hare foot, a beaver-gnawed piece of wood . . . well, you know what I mean. I don't have a great deal of this stuff, mind you, but I do have *some.* Reminders of wandering out there along the shores of time. (The moose teeth I have here—for a necklace?—remind me of that day we were on the Alagnak River and it had been pouring for hours and were we ever cold.)

But I have had increasing problems with this collecting bit in the last two or three years. If I lived permanently out there, the collected stuff would nevertheless be in the original context and that would be fine. On my desk, however, that moose mandible is not looking right these days. I really think it wants to go back. And I think the rock scallop shells want to go back. And the pumice. It's very difficult to get at, but so far I understand at least two things; the collected items just do not belong out of the original context, and contrary to what has so often been suggested, I no longer believe I am kept in touch with out there by having that moose mandible down here. In fact, I am beginning to believe the reverse.

In other words, when I drag that old mandible away from the wild and bring it down here, I am putting it in a cage. I *think* it's the same as putting a brown bear in a zoo or stuffing a fish and hanging it on the wall. So instead of denying myself the chance to be in touch with these bits of the universe by leaving them in original context, I am denying myself the chance by bringing them home. This all began to make sense to me when I realized it is the collective primeval memories I want to try to get at rather than a series of recent individual episodes which are not very important. And while I need more time to understand what I am talking about, I already know for sure what direction the collected items are going to go. Back out there. I am going to take them all back, but when I set them down again in the wilderness I'll not be saying goodbye. No. I'll be saying hello, and by that time maybe I'll understand better what the hello means.

Meanwhile, that moose tooth necklace. I might go ahead with that, wear it occasionally and see if the same problem crops up, and then eventually put it back, too. Or am I rationalizing? Should the moose teeth go back now, along with the rest?

We came off the mountain in scorching sun and were glad when the local star finally dropped below the peaks about nine o'clock. The next morning was overcast but the rain held off. When we reached the small lake there was a bull moose standing in the water—near the other side. We traversed the shoreline quietly but otherwise made no attempt to be discreet. When we were roughly opposite him, he came forward about fifty feet, watching intently. At the near end of the lake, now just out of his view behind a knoll, we set down the packs and I decided to try some photographs, if he would have no particular objection. This was my fourth season in the Katmai, and from the beginning I had hoped to spend a few minutes with a moose, somewhere out there, in circumstances under which both parties would feel reasonably comfortable. That is, I never had any intention of stalking such an animal nor of pushing in until flight distance was violated. But I wanted to be close enough to have a conversation.

   When the camera was ready, I walked slowly and quietly up on the little knoll, and then forward about six yards. I suppose he and I were now one hundred feet apart. He stayed where he was and so did I. After five or six frames, I went back and changed rolls, shouldered the pack and started to leave. But I hadn't *talked* to him. So I dropped the pack, retrieved the camera and returned to my spot. He was still there, munching some bottom grass, and I proceeded to talk to him for about twenty minutes. I urged him to come on over and say hello, and while now and then he shuffled around a bit, he never came closer. Every time I talked he twitched his ears. Every so often he snorted almost inaudibly but I sensed no malice. Of course, had it been rutting season I would not have been foolish enough to expose myself where cover was a few one-foot-high willows.

   He continued to munch, shuffle, snort, and twitch ears when spoken to. Finally I thanked him and said goodbye. As I shouldered the pack, I thought about the possibility that some of the pictures might be more than just a moose standing in a lake, but I also knew the consideration was secondary. What counted was that I had finally talked with a moose at one hundred feet for twenty minutes under apparently relaxed ground rules.

   When I walked away, an even more important realization dawned. I knew I had been seeing that moose as Katmai; far more than a moose. I was really beginning to *feel* he was a volcano, or a willow bush or the peak we had just climbed. And vice versa. So his boundary—that is, where his body meets the space around him—had begun to blur. After years of knowing how utterly specific wildlife photography has been, in Katmai I had finally sensed the generalization; that a moose is not a moose and is made of stardust. Could I show that in a photograph? Probably not, although I wondered. But in a book? With enough approaches at my disposal, would it be possible to get across to someone else the idea that a moose is a volcano?

At the far end of the Valley of Ten Thousand Smokes, in late August of 1977, I met David Affelder and enjoyed several long talks with him. He had come to Katmai alone but traveled into the valley itself with two other people. During our conversations, David talked at some length about one or two of his earlier backpacking trips, but he said nothing about the walk he had just completed. (It was only several days later that I learned David had exhibited considerable fear when stream crossings were encountered on his way through the valley. Glacier-fed streams, creeks, and rivers are almost always dangerous to ford, although I think far too many hikers are not sufficiently aware of the potential for disaster. And anyone who is truly fearful of such crossings should never attempt them alone. When the water volume is high, after heavy rains or at mid-day because of runoff, a slight error in judgment can quickly—indeed, almost instantaneously—build to a no-return situation.)

When Affelder came over to the smallest hut to say goodbye the next morning, he seemed in a great hurry to leave because he wanted to catch a certain flight back to Anchorage. I cautioned him about "hurrying" in such country, and I reminded him that the rivers were going to be up; it had rained savagely the previous day, and the sky said more rain was about to come. But David was ready to go, period.

By 11:00 that morning, which was just about when Affelder would have reached the River Lethe, it was blowing hard and raining like hell. I remember thinking about David's clothing. He had told me he did not believe in down equipment (the "warmest" item he had with him, other than a sweater, was a bluejean jacket), and the only rain gear he was carrying was a poncho, which is terribly inadequate if there is wind along with the rain.

The following day, I tried to leave the valley with another person, though I did not really think we would be able to cross the Lethe. There had been too much rain. As we reached that swift, muddy, glacier-fed river that originates under the shadow of Mageik the volcano, it was immediately apparent that an attempt to ford would be suicidal. And then, simultaneously, we both caught sight of an orange something, in the water downstream and just at the edge of the Lethe's sixty-foot-sheer drop into the great flume. A backpack? Yes, it was a backpack and it belonged to David Affelder.

The wind was coming up, but we wanted to cache David's pack and, although there was virtually no chance, I felt we had to check out the slim possibility of a crossing upstream. All this consumed two hours or more, it was already noon, the wind had reached about thirty-five knots, and one of those huge Valley of Ten Thousand Smokes duststorms was upon us. It would have been idiocy to strike for the huts, against the wind and blinded by dust. We could not have made it, and I knew thirty-five knots wasn't the end of it. There is no shelter anywhere on the floor of the valley and a tent won't hold, but there is a small "sand" bank at the ford where we had cached David's pack, enough of a bank to cut windforce by, say, fifteen percent. As we dropped downstream again toward this spot, I realized we were about to commit ourselves to a nest; that is, we were not going to be moving *anywhere* for quite awhile. We had very few minutes left during which to choose this nest and, once having made the choice, we were going to have to sit out there and take it and we had better be intelligent about it. I was certain we were going to catch sixty-mile-an-hour winds, and we would have to figure out how to survive the night, if it came to that, without normal shelter.

Well, the wind reached sixty, and we sat there and learned how it feels to be violently sandblasted for hours. By late afternoon it was time to find out if we could rig a cocoon for the night. Using one of the two tents we had, plus the backpacks, we made a survival bubble and were able to withdraw from direct contact with the howling winds and dust. Had the night come, we could have made it through, with or without rain. But at 6:00 in the evening the frenzy started to abate, and by 7:00, with the wind at twenty-five knots and dropping, we broke out for the walk back to the huts.

There were several others at that end of the Valley, and they had all talked with Affelder on previous days. Thus, we had to convey the tragic news that David had almost certainly drowned in River Lethe. As we conveyed this sadness, it was dusk and the wind was almost gone. The mist shrouding the Aleutian Range was starting to lift. There in the Valley of Ten Thousand Smokes we were shortly going to experience absolute silence.

A few minutes later, I went over to the tiniest of the huts and, as dusk left and night came, lit a candle for David Affelder.

*River Lethe: The Valley of
Ten Thousand Smokes, August 1973.*

Windy Creek, Knife Creek, and the River Lethe meet at Three Forks to become the Ukak River. Here, the Ukak is thundering in flood at the lower end of the Valley of Ten Thousand Smokes, just before it turns the last cliffs of the 1912 ashflow, and heads northeast and north for ten miles to join the Savonoski River.

On the following pages, the early stages of one of the valley's great duststorms; then Baked Mountain under the snow summits of Trident and Falling Mountain, with River Lethe's gorge in the foreground . . .

. . . and finally, at the base of Mageik—the headwaters of River Lethe from the air.

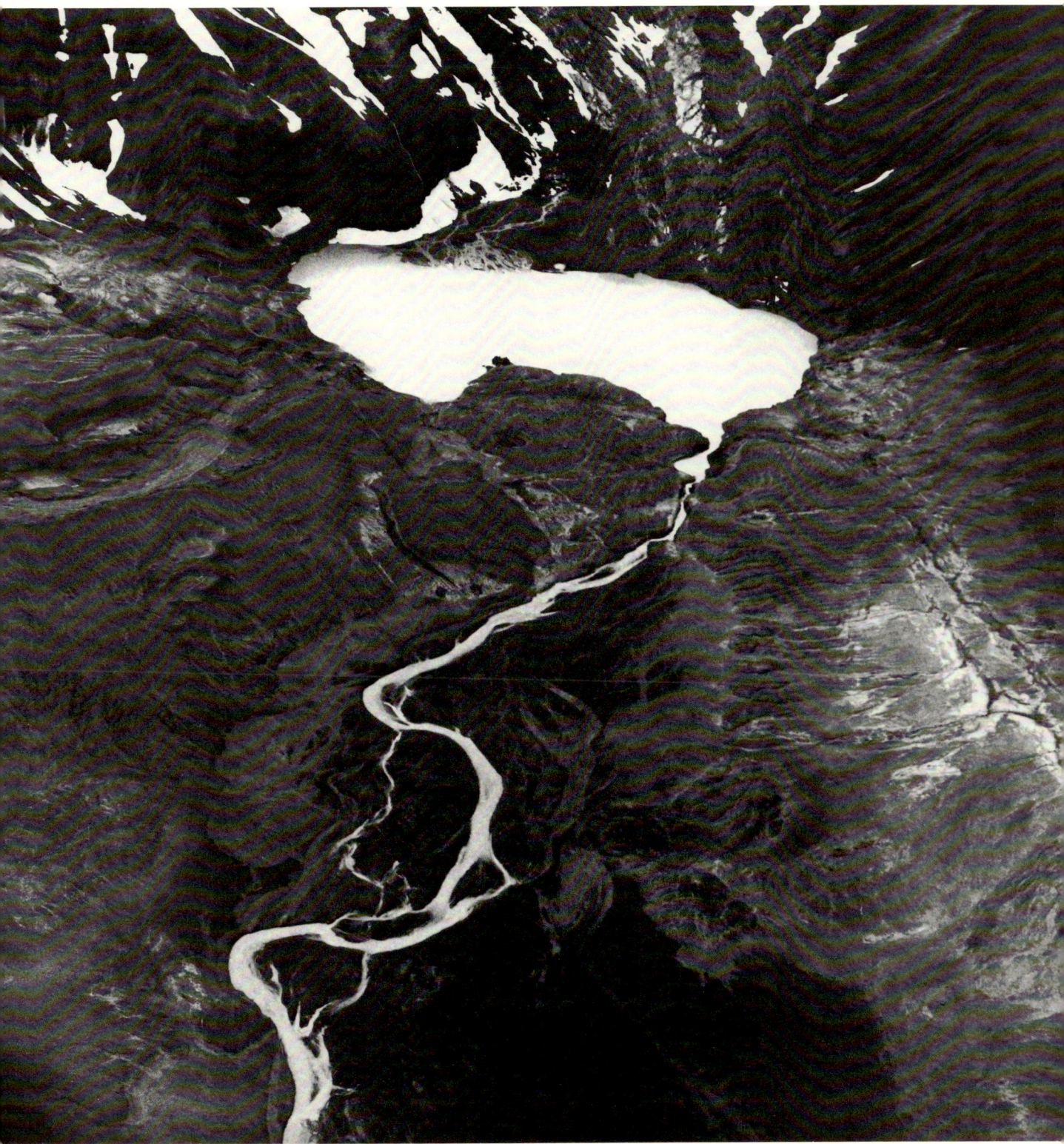

Yesterday afternoon there were some crows over on the point making an appalling racket endlessly. They're gone tonight.
   Those crows come in as tide starts to recede. Mostly there are about six of them. They pick around the high water line and caw incessantly at each other. Several times I spoke to them about the racket they were making, but they did not
seem to care.

Clouds are massed above the peaks and the sun is leaving. Now the wind is dropping and tide recedes. There are ten seagulls on the beach not making a sound. They just flew off not making a sound. Except wingbeats.

Another unheard of cloudless day in the Katmai, this one beginning with pink fog on Naknek Lake at 6:00 a.m.

Enormous dark land today. The rain should be along soon.

Great brooding wild land. Your winds and storms and unceasing suddenness of wind and cloud and rain and storm and clearing. Wind. Always the wind.

But I remember a night when an almost-full moon rose over La Gorce in clear and windless sky. Naknek Lake was sixty miles of glass and that may not happen again for half a century.

One planet floated above the Katolinat summit. Streaks of moonlight far out on the water.

Fox wolf bear moose eagle tracks on the beach alongside salmon stream this morning. Slight fog. Brooks Lake is glass. So quiet.

Ikagluik the mountain will be under full moon tonight. I heard a loon calling. Now the loon just called again.

At Fure's cabin.

It was near dark one evening when I heard the loon just mentioned. I was standing at water's edge below Fure's cabin, surrounded by immense, absolutely total silence. Ikagluik the mountain was rising under full moon. Then the call from that bird up there. And then once again.

Fure's cabin is one of those wilderness works of art. Roy Fure built it along about 1926. Roy trapped, hunted, and fished, and plied Naknek Lake for years in his various boats—especially the sail-powered, Bristol Bay double ender, which is just a skeleton now as it rots into the sand. But the cabin is no skeleton. After more than fifty years it stands virtually as solid as rock. Magnificent hand-hewn beams and logs. Fine corner work, proportions that ring true throughout. And inside . . . the color of the wood has darkened to a deep red-brown.

   I owe a debt to this cabin or, I should say, to Roy Fure. I have done some writing there while the gale brought torrential rain, and I have also done some writing there when the inestimable silence was just beyond four walls. Those hours are burned into memory; holed up in a monument to one man's skill and caring. Roy died more than ten years before I reached the Katmai. Otherwise, had I been able to meet and talk with him, I feel certain I would have written the story of man and cabin.

On the evening I have mentioned, when I stopped writing and walked out into dusky silence to stand at water's edge and twice hear the loon, I suspected stillness would last the night through and dawn would arrive shrouded. So I rose early and went down to the water again. Eventually the mists started to dissipate. Ikagluik slowly became visible, a dark form with its two summits—and then finally the whiteness of Mt. Griggs on high.

A short story (sometimes a long one) could be written about virtually every photograph between these covers. While a great deal, if not all, of what I have said on preceding pages is the attempted translation of something I saw out there, across one hundred and fifty-three pages I have mostly refrained from speaking directly about the photographs. Well, I sense page one hundred and seventy-six closing in on me, so before saying my goodbyes to the Katmai, I want to tell just a few stories. The photographs are only symbols, of course, but I want to go back through the symbol and touch again those secret hours when I was out there with camera, in the wind and space.

Wind. Always the wind. Must have been a thirty-five knot gale blowing when I photographed the Balsam poplar on page 87. I couldn't hold very steady, but the air was moving and the poplars were moving so who was I to worry about holding steady? But can one photograph *wind*? I really don't know. In the Katmai, I tried not a few times to do just that, but I am not convinced it is possible.

And the robin's nest (page 170). Yes, this is the nest I talked about on page 85. I made the photograph in 1975, but since then have returned four or five times to say hello, to quietly remember the more than two hours I originally spent with the nest, during the first hour of which I was merely trying to get the damn camera where I wanted it—without busting the tree or damaging the nest or trampling the moss underneath the tree. Well there it is—or, at least the symbol. I got what I was after. But what was I after? Did I come away with anything more than a reminiscence?

On page 16 there is evidence of a porcupine in a tree. I was poking along the shore when I spied the critter up there. I put the long lens on the camera so I could keep my distance, but even so he or she turned his or her tail at me. I made the photograph and departed quickly, but I remember how frustrated I was because the animal had faced away from me . . . until a day or so later, when I realized that porcupine-in-tree turned hind end is quintessential porcupine.

On page 70 is one of my favorite trees in the Katmai. It is a dead white spruce, with a now-abandoned bald eagle nest on top. (This is the same tree that appears with fledglings on page 71, photographed in 1974. The following year the adult eagles relocated about a mile away.) But in 1974, while coasting the shoreline about three hundred yards from the fledglings, I heard one of the adults call from at least a half mile beyond the nest. I had never before heard this particular call. It was not distress, it was not a greeting. But the cry had an imperative to it. I reached for the binoculars. Again the cry from distant hillside. And now the fledglings stood, stretching and flapping, each to one edge of the nest. They were being called to wing, but were not ready. A few hours, a day or two . . . it was *almost* time for them.

I know it is a bit hard to make out, but that is a moose rack and skull on page 159. It is an old friend, and appears on pages 18 and 164 as well. When I went back to visit a year after the original photographs were made, it was underwater, partially green with algae and partially covered with silt. In other words, my friend was returning to the shifting sands, and the next time I visit will very probably have disappeared.

 This visiting of old friends out there is all very well, but one must remember that changes can be rapid in this country. At the end of long miles, the friend may be gone, overwhelmed by suddenness from torrential rain, flood, gigantic wind, landslide . . . or, as with the moose rack underwater and my abandoned eagle-nest-tree, a slower return to those shifting, unpredictable sands.

Early in the first week of August, 1975, I returned to the far end of the Valley of Ten Thousand Smokes, having spent eight days alone there in 1973. (A pilgrimage. Those old friends again. In this case the peaks, the space, and yes—the valley's great winds. And the same pilgrimage in 1976 and again in 1977.) In the evening of that first day, after eleven miles under full pack, I was on the shoulder of Baked Mountain, about 1200' above the floor of the valley. Dinner was getting cold and I was famished and tired as hell. But I was watching the *holes* in the fast-moving clouds overhead. Because wherever a hole, a corresponding patch of sun moving across the land.

About a mile east of me was an extraordinary snowpatch on the lower slopes of Broken Mountain, but those slopes were a very dark gray at that moment. From the south, however, a sunpatch was advancing in my general direction, and was it going to illuminate that piece of landscape-with-snowpatch? In my travels with camera I have never been one to wait on the light, but for this occasion I changed my own rules. I stretched full length on the ground, propped my elbows—and waited. Shortly, as the little piece of sunlight transformed yonder hillside in my groundglass, I exposed the one frame I had time for.

For some minutes thereafter, I watched the little piece of sunlight move on down the valley, and then I got up and went to dinner, so to speak. As for the photograph I made, it appears on page 26.

Just one more "story." That brown bear on page 57. Everyone who has discussed that photograph with me wants to know how close to the bear I was. About sixty feet, as I recall. That is fairly close, to be sure, but the important point is that I made myself quite visible to the bear long before proximity was a consideration. The bear did not seem inclined to alter direction as a result of my presence—in fact, seemed very unconcerned—so I stayed put with almost no misgivings.

Subsequently, I have often wished I could go back and ask the subject whether he thinks this photograph says more about bear than about me.

At the beginning of these years in Katmai, in the first of the field journals, I wondered whether it is "possible to stop photographing, yet continue to use the camera to stop photographing with?" Thus, the desire to completely transcend the camera while continuing to use it. This lack of conscious contact with the "subject" matter, through the groundglass of the camera, intrigues me. I am now suggesting (to myself) that there is a recognition of kinship, an isolating recognition that takes place first, well before the camera is reached for. But this recognition must include the separateness of whatever the subject of the moment is. Treeness, etc. In other words, I have been asking myself, in the last few years, whether or not it is possible to photograph the unique *awareness* that a tree or a bear has? (My own awareness of a bear moving across the landscape is not very significant, when it comes to the photograph. Such photographs cannot be anything more than autobiographical.)

For the sake of argument, suppose I get closer and closer to expressing in a photograph the tree's awareness. Could this mean that the closer I get to that point, the greater the possibility of ceasing to photograph? I would think it could mean that.

I didn't want to leave. So wild out there, the peaks and glaciers and the magnificent Angle Creek valley far below. I made the photographs, huddled at the base of an outcrop on the steep sidehill. Then I put away the camera and walked back up into the wind, which must have been blowing about thirty knots. In fact, I damn near lost my knit cap as I headed across the ridge for the dropoff to Windy Creek. Before going over the side, I turned and said goodbye to the peaks west, goodbye to Katmai . . . and a wave of acknowledgment, kinship, a thank you. There were some tears, but the stiff wind blew them away as I started the descent.

Epilogue

One of these days, I kept telling myself, I would move out from Brooks Camp without the cameras, at last. I finally did it. Left them behind and headed beyond tundra hills for a mountain lake—the Tarn. The first time without cameras in twenty years of wilderness. It was the end of August, and this was to be the concluding field trip for what I had been trying to find out in five summers of rambles across Katmai's wild. But I soon realized the visit was not final anything. *This* visit was in some other realm. Time did not pass, but hovered somewhere nearby. For just those two days, why had time's arrow stopped at the edge of an enchanted tarn? I am not certain. Maybe I'll know more later on. For now, I am content to leave it at that . . . but if tomorrow I were told that if I never physically revisited the Katmai, a five-year-old could, twenty years from now, go in there alone and see it wild and free of manipulation . . . I would need to breathe deeply and might reach for a stiff one, but I like to think I could make the decision in favor of the child, and rather quickly.

Acknowledgments

It all started on a cold evening in the middle of winter in Glacier Bay. Tom Ritter (at that time, Chief of Interpretation for USNPS in Alaska) dropped a pebble in my pond by quietly suggesting I should get out to southwestern Alaska and make acquaintance with Katmai National Monument. If there were any ripples that night, they were imperceptible. But several months later, Tom's intensity regarding the Katmai started to unsettle me, because he had left so much unsaid in his approach to the subject. As ripples became more and more evident, I finally had to go and understand, if possible, what was lurking beneath Tom Ritter's intuition. I went and have not yet recovered and do not expect to. The blame is squarely at Tom's feet. He started this and I do not intend to let him forget that.

Throughout my efforts in the Katmai, USNPS personnel were unfailingly cooperative, and many of them gave me the benefit of hours of their time discussing the monument with me. My thanks to: Stan Albright (former state director), Richard Prasil, Bob Peterson, Judith Ayres, Jim Luthy, Ralph Furbush, JoAnne Clark Popham, Mike Shapsnikoff, Jim and Carol Hepburn, Steve and Lisa Buskirk, John Dennis, Deanne Adams, and the USNPS receptionists in King Salmon—Wilma McElhaney, Jean Patterson, Patty Wood, Debi Tibbetts. And, in spite of my stomach, I think back fondly on those superb low-level photographic flights taken with Will Troyer, management biologist for USNPS in Alaska. I would also like to express my appreciation to John A. Hussey, former National Park Service historian, for his magnificent document, "Embattled Katmai: A History of Katmai National Monument," printed by the Department of the Interior in 1971.

Originally I had intended to include the "entire" Katmai bibliography to date (more than three hundred entries) but after months of reflection on this aspect, it seemed apparent that such an extensive list would not serve the general reader. Compilation of a selected bibliography in the earth and life sciences was aided immeasurably by opinions from Don Dumond, Department of Anthropology,

University of Oregon, and at the University of Alaska—Fred Dean, program leader of the Biology and Resource Management section of the Cooperative Park Studies Unit, and Jürgen Kienle of the Geophysical Institute.

I am very grateful for the opportunities I had to fraternize at the concessioner end of the Brooks Camp community, for this put me in the unique position of being able to discuss the differences of opinion and concept that naturally exist between USNPS and Wien Air Alaska's Brooks Lodge operation. I trust I never betrayed any confidence on either side of that rather low fence. My thanks, then, to concessioner staff *in toto,* and especially Curt Roe, Gary and Judith Anderson, Bertha Folden—and the inimitable Bruce Jones, for our periodic free-wheeling, free-swinging, two-hour conversations with the Chivas Regal at hand.

Personal thanks to long-time friends Fred Rothchild, who helped so much with the 1975 field season, and Chuck Janda for loan of photographic equipment; to the John H. Murray family for their permission to reproduce the Lake Walker painting; to Elizabeth Mills, JoAnne Clark Popham, Mark Schrader, and Mike Tollefson for their willingness to contribute to this book; to George Tilser for his gracious presentation of a tent after mine had been wiped out by a brown bear; and to Susi and Mike Tollefson and Barbara Blinn, USNPS at Brooks Camp, for hospitality, support, and discussion.

Also personal thanks to William Schwarz for his detailed and invaluable critical commentary on the manuscript, and for his perceptive criticisms and suggestions on layout. It is not possible to overestimate the importance of this friend's role in the final juggling of the pieces in this book. And to Noel Young at Capra Press, for his long-term faith in this project.

And a unique debt of gratitude is owed Carolyn Elder, who traveled so many miles with me and who knows better than I do what the Katmai is.

As for Gil Blinn, superintendent, Katmai National Monument; his support in the field was of incalculable value, and while I understand my debt, I do not know how to write it down. Gil's unswerving cooperation and friendship were the keys to the five field seasons, and the only way I can repay what he gave me is to give it back to the Katmai. Again, that remains to be seen.

*Mama sow's tracks,
Naknek Lake, 1974.*

Bibliography

The entries listed below were selected in an attempt to provide the reader with an in-depth survey of literature of the Katmai National Monument, since a "complete" bibliography would include more than 300 items.

PREHISTORY

Clark, G. H., 1977. Archaeology on the Alaska Peninsula: The Coast of Shelikof Strait, 1963–1965. U. of Oregon Anthropological Papers 13, Eugene: 247 pp.

Davis, W. A., 1954. Archaeological Investigations of Inland and Coastal Sites of the Katmai National Monument, Alaska. Rep't to the NPS, U. of Oregon, Eugene. Archives of Archaeology, Micro-card No. 4, publ. by the Soc. for Am. Archaeology and the U. of Wisconsin Press, Madison: 205 pp.

Dumond, D. E., 1964. Archaeological Survey in Katmai National Monument, Alaska: 1963. Final Rep't to NPS, Contract 14-10-0434-947, Dep't. of Anthropology, U. of Oregon, Eugene: 47 pp. (At NPS library, King Salmon.)

———, 1965. Archaeological Survey in Katmai National Monument, Alaska: 1964. Final Rep't. to NPS, Contract 14-10-0434-1492, Dep't. of Anthropology, U. of Oregon, Eugene: 50 pp. (At NPS library, King Salmon.)

———, 1971. A Summary of Archaeology in the Katmai Region, Southwestern Alaska. U. of Oregon Anthropological Papers 2, Eugene: 61 pp.

———, 1972. The Alaska Peninsula in Alaskan Prehistory, *in* For the Chief: Essays in Honor of Luther S. Cressman, F. W. Voget and R. L. Stephenson, eds. U. of Oregon Anthropological Papers 4, Eugene: 29-47.

———, 1974. Prehistoric Dwellings in Katmai National Monument, Alaska, *in* Nat. Geog. Soc. Rep'ts., 1967 Projects. Nat. Geog. Soc., Wash., D. C.: 57-70.

———, 1977. The Eskimos and Aleuts. Thames and Hudson, London: 180 pp.

———, W. Henn, and R. Stuckenrath, 1976. Archaeology and Prehistory of the Alaska Peninsula. Anthropological Papers of the U. of Alaska 18 (1), Fairbanks: 17-29.

Heusser, C. J., 1963. Postglacial Palynology and Archaeology in the Naknek River Drainage Area, Alaska. Am. Antiquity 29 (1): 74-81.

Oswalt, W. H., 1955. Prehistoric Sea Mammal Hunters at Kaflia, Alaska. Anthropological Papers of the U. of Alaska 4 (1), Fairbanks: 22-61.

Shields, H. M., 1977. Salvage Archaeology in Katmai National Monument, 1974. Occasional Paper No. 2, Anthropology and Hist. Preservation, Alaska Cooperative Pk. Studies Unit, U. of Alaska, Fairbanks: 16 pp.

HISTORY

Anon., 1919. The Ten Thousand Smokes Now a National Monument. Nat. Geog. Mag. 35 (4): 359-366.

Davis, W. A., 1961. Mt. Katmai, Alaska, Eruption: A Transcript of a Tape Recording with Eyewitnesses of 1912 Eruption. U. of Oregon, Eugene: 24 pp., typescript. (At NPS library, King Salmon.)

Griggs, R. F., 1917. The Valley of Ten Thousand Smokes: National Geographic Society Explorations in the Katmai District of Alaska. Nat. Geog. Mag. 31 (1): 13-68. (The expeditions of 1915 and 1916, led by Griggs.)

———, 1918. The Valley of Ten Thousand Smokes: An Account of the Discovery and Exploration of the Most Wonderful Volcanic Region in the World. Nat. Geog. Mag. 33 (2): 115-169. (The expedition of 1917, led by Griggs.)

———, 1921. Our Greatest National Monument: The National Geographic Society Completes its Explorations in the Valley of Ten Thousand Smokes. Nat. Geog. Mag. 40 (3): 219-292. (The expedition of 1919, led by Griggs.)

———, 1922. The Valley of Ten Thousand Smokes. Nat. Geog. Soc., Wash., D. C.: 341 pp.

Hussey, J. A., 1971. Embattled Katmai: A History of Katmai National Monument. Off. of History and Hist. Architecture, Western Service Ctr., NPS: 457 pp. (This is the major historical work on Katmai NM; detailed to 1918, summarized 1918–1954.)

Kauffman, J. M., 1954. Katmai National Monument, Alaska: A History of its Establishment and Revision of its Boundaries. NPS: 37 pp., mimeo. (At NPS library, King Salmon.)

Martin, G. C., 1913. The Recent Eruption of Katmai Volcano in Alaska. Nat. Geog. Mag. 24 (2): 131-181. (Martin conducts interviews and makes observations while on Shelikof Strait, beginning just four weeks after the eruption.)

McDonald, L., 1962. Robert Moran's Fleet Braved Alaskan Seas, Moran's Sternwheeler Fleet ran into Troubled Waters, Moran's Sternwheelers go on to the Upper Yukon. The Seattle *Times*, March 25, April 1, 8. (Sternwheeler fleet in Katmai Bay, June 1898.)

[Perry, Cap't. K. W.], 1912. Volcanoes of Alaska. Nat. Geog. Mag. 23 (8): 824-832. (Extract from rep't. of Cap't. Perry of Revenue Cutter *Manning*; first in the series of articles on the eruption of 1912 and subsequent Society-sponsored expeditions to the area.)

Tollefson, M. J., 1975. Interview with Father Harry Kaiakokonok and George Kosbruk, Interview with Father Harry Kaiakokonok: Eyewitness Accounts of the Katmai Eruption. NPS: 34 pp., typescript. (At NPS library, King Salmon.)

NARRATIVES

Beach, R., 1940. Personal Exposures. Harper & Bros., N. Y.: 62-69.

Hubbard, B. R., 1935. Cradle of the Storms. Dodd, Mead & Co., N. Y.: 167-272.

Petroff [Petrov], I., 1881. Alaska's Census: Conclusion of Mr. Petroff's Enumerating Journey. New York *Herald*, January 11: p. 5, columns 4-5. (Second of two articles.)

Shanz, A. B., 1891. Our Alaska Expedition . . . VIII. Frank Leslie's Illustrated Newspaper, November 28: 268 and 274. (Final of eight articles.)

Sumner, L., 1952. Magnificent Katmai. Sierra Club Bulletin 37 (10): 29-51. (Sumner was with the NPS Alaska Recreation Survey of 1951.)

Tilton, Captain G. F., 1928. "Cap'n George Fred" Himself. Doubleday, Doran; N. Y.: 290-293.

Wadsworth, G., 1972 (February). Katmai's Wild Horse. Alaska Magazine: p. 31.

EARTH SCIENCES

Curtis, G. H., 1968. The Stratigraphy of the Ejecta from the 1912 Eruption of Mount Katmai and Novarupta, Alaska, *in* Studies in Volcanology, R. R. Coats, R. L. Hay, and C. A. Anderson, eds. Geol. Soc. Am. Memoir 116: 153-210.

Fenner, C. N., 1920. The Katmai Region, Alaska, and the Great Eruption of 1912. Jour. Geol. 28 (7): 569-606.

———, 1923. The Origin and Mode of Emplacement of the Great Tuff Deposit of the Valley of Ten Thousand Smokes. Nat. Geog. Soc. Contributed Tech. Papers, Katmai Series 1 (1): 74 pp.

———, 1926. The Katmai Magmatic Province. Jour. Geol. 35 (7, pt. 2): 673-772.

Kienle, J., 1970. Gravity Traverses in the Valley of Ten Thousand Smokes, Katmai National Monument, Alaska. Jour. Geophysical Res. 75 (32): 6641-6649.

Kubota, S. and E. Berg, 1967. Evidence for Magma in the Katmai Volcanic Range. Bull. volcanologique 31: 175-214.

MacGregor, A. G., 1952. Eruptive Mechanisms: Mt. Pelée, the Soufrière of St. Vincent and the Valley of Ten Thousand Smokes. Bull. volcanologique 12: 49-74.

Martin, G. C., 1913. See under *History*.

Matumoto, T., 1971. Seismic Body Waves Observed in the Vicinity of Mount Katmai, Alaska, and Evidence for the Existence of Molten Chambers. Geol. Soc. Am. Bull. 82 (10): 2905-2920.

Muller, E. H., 1952. Glacial History of the Naknek District, Alaska Peninsula, Alaska (abstract). Geol. Soc. Am. Bull. 63 (12, pt. 2): 1284.

Oswalt, W. H., 1957. Volcanic Activity and Alaskan Spruce Growth in A. D. 1783. Science 126: 928-929.

Snyder, G. L., 1954. Eruption of Trident Volcano, Katmai National Monument, Alaska, February-June, 1953. Geol. Survey Circ. 318: 7 pp.

Spurr, J. E., 1900. A Reconnaissance in Southwestern Alaska in 1898. Geol. Survey 20th Ann'l. Rep't., Pt. 7: 31-264.

Zies, E. G., 1929. The Valley of 10,000 Smokes: I. The Fumarolic Incrustations and their Bearing on Ore Deposition. II. The Acid Gases Contributed to the Sea During Volcanic Activity. Nat. Geog. Soc. Contributed Tech. Papers, Katmai Series 1 (4): 79 pp.

PLANTS

Cameron, R. E., 1970. Soil Microbial Ecology of the Valley of Ten Thousand Smokes, Alaska. Jour. Arizona Acad. Sci. 6 (1): 11-40.

Griggs, R. F., 1919. The Beginnings of Revegetation in Katmai Valley. Ohio Jour. Sci. 19: 318-342.

———, 1933. The Colonization of the Katmai Ash, a New and Inorganic "Soil." Am. Jour. Botany 20: 92-113.

———, 1936. The Vegetation of the Katmai District. Ecology 17: 380-417.

Hultén, E., 1937. Outline of the History of Arctic and Boreal Biota during the Quarternary Period. Bokförlags A. B. Thule, Stockholm: 168 pp.

———, 1968. Flora of Alaska and Neighboring Territories; A Manual of the Vascular Plants. Stanford U. Press, Stanford, Cal.: 1008 pp. (Not specific to Katmai, but is an important synthesis.)

Viereck, L. A., and E. L. Little, Jr., 1972. Alaska Trees and Shrubs. Agriculture Handbk. No. 410, Forest Serv., Dep't. of Agr., Wash., D. C.: 265 pp.

BIRDS AND MAMMALS

Cahalane, V. H., 1959. A Biological Survey of Katmai National Monument, Smithsonian Misc. Coll. 138 (5), Wash., D. C.: 246 pp.

Gabrielson, I. N., and F. C. Lincoln, 1959. The Birds of Alaska. The Stackpole Co., Harrisburg, Pa., and the Wildlife Management Inst., Wash., D. C.: 922 pp. (Not specific to Katmai, but is an important synthesis.)

Kessel, B., and D. D. Gibson, 1978. Status and Distribution of Alaska Birds. Studies in Avian Biology No. 1, Cooper Ornithological Soc., U. C. Los Angeles: 100 pp. (Not specific to Katmai, but is an important synthesis.)

Murie, O. J., 1959. Fauna of the Aleutian Islands and Alaska Peninsula. N. Am. Fauna Ser. No. 61, Fish and Wildlife Serv., Dep't. of Int., Wash., D. C.: 406 pp.

Schiller, E. L., and R. Rausch, 1956. Mammals of the Katmai National Monument, Arctic 9 (3): 191-201.

FISHERIES AND LIMNOLOGY

Buck, E. H., C. Bowden, J. Baldridge, and W. J. Wilson, 1978. Bibliography, Synthesis, and Modeling of Naknek River Aquatic System Information. Unpubl. rep't. for PNWR, NPS, Arctic Environmental Inf. and Data Ctr., U. of Alaska, Anchorage: 244 pp.

Heard, W. R., R. L. Wallace, and W. L. Hartman, 1969. Distributions of Fishes in Fresh Water of Katmai National Monument, Alaska, and their Zoogeographical Implications. Fish and Wildlife Serv., Dep't. of Int., Special Scientific Rep't.—Fisheries 590: 20 pp.

Kavanaugh, R., 1978. Comments—Ross Kavanagh [sic]—11/24/78, "Bibliography, Synthesis, and Modeling of Naknek River Aquatic System Information." File memo, Alaska Area Off., NPS, Anchorage: 4 pp., mimeo.

GENERAL

Alaska Planning Group, 1974. Final Environmental Statement. Proposed Katmai National Park, Alaska. Dep't. of Int., Wash., D. C.: 652 pp. (At NPS library, King Salmon.)

Selkregg, L L., ed., n.d. Alaska Regional Profiles: Southwest Region. Off. of the Governor, State of Alaska, and the Joint Federal-State Land Use Planning Comm. for Alaska: 313 pp. (At NPS library, King Salmon.)

*Five thousand copies were printed
by Haagen Printing, Santa Barbara, in
August 1979. Typography by Graham Mackintosh.
Binding by Cardoza-James, San Francisco.
Design by the author.*

*A limited edition of twenty-six copies,
lettered A to Z, was signed by
the author and included an
original photographic
print of the Katmai.*